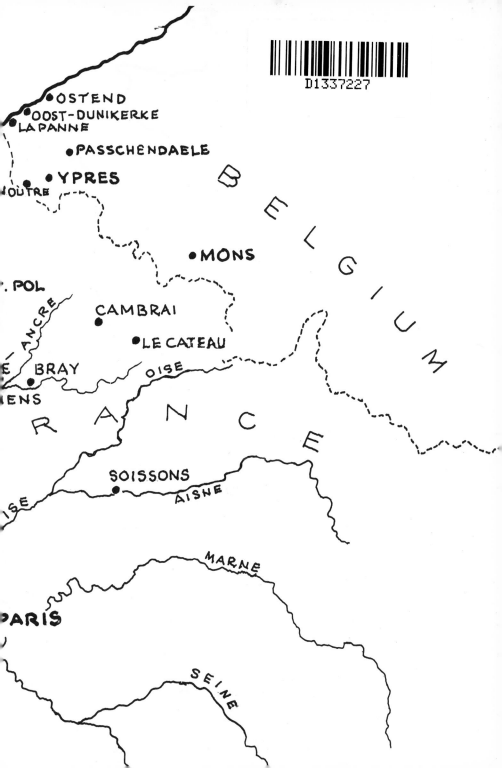

FROM HELL
TO THE
HIMALAYAS

From Hell
To The
Himalayas

Colonel C.F. Hodgson

King & Wilks
Publishers

King & Wilks (Pty) Ltd.
Publishers
109 Matruh Building
Westville Road, Westville 3630

P.O. Box 525
Westville 3630
South Africa.

ISBN 0 - 620 - 06241 - X

Typesetting by Kwikset, Durban
Reprographic by Photoplate, Durban
Printed by Interprint, Durban

To Rhoda, who gave me the inspiration to write this book and the determination to see it through — my heartfelt thanks.

My grateful and sincere thanks to Gladys Marion Parry who encouraged me to persevere, and also to Jill Hardy, Coo-Coo Wall, Lois Martin Povall and Daphne Child for everything they did to help me.

CONTENTS

The author wishes to acknowledge the South African National Museum of Military History for the use of photographs in their possession of conditions at the front in World War I.

The author also wishes to acknowledge The Daily News, Durban, for permission to use a photograph of the Himalayas.

All other photographs published in the book are from the author's personal collection.

1

Le Cateau

They called us "Saturday night soldiers." This was the label given to us chaps in the Territorial Army — commonly known as "Terriers" — as we used to do our training mostly at weekends.

It was all a bit of a lark for us lads of the village and a bit of cheap entertainment for Saturday nights. No one took it very seriously and, in that unusually good English summer of 1914, the thought of war never entered our heads.

Came August of 1914, some chap was assassinated in Yugoslavia, and before you could say "Form fours", England was at war. The Regular Army was mobilised and on its way to France. We "Terriers" were not liable for overseas service, but owing to the small size of the Regular Army, any volunteers were gladly accepted. So it was that by the end of the month, and "wet behind the ears", I found myself in France as a 2nd lieutenant in charge of a section of field artillery. The British Army had already suffered its first defeat and was retreating from Mons.

My first experience of real fighting was at a place called Le Cateau, near Cambrai. The day before the battle we moved up to an assembly point near Le Cateau where we were to be addressed by General Sir Horace Smith-Dorrien, who was our 2nd Corps Commander. He described the general situation and told us that the British Expeditionary Force was in retreat and that the position was very serious. Smith-Dorrien then gave us a pep talk and said that our regiment, plus certain infantry battalions, had been chosen to cover the retreat of the main forces falling back from Mons. He again emphasised the gravity of the situation and said: "So much depends on you and there must be no retreat. It is do or die."

To us young chaps, most of us aged about eighteen or nineteen, this all sounded very exciting and had the most stimulating effect. It made us feel that the fate of the whole B.E.F. depended on us. I often wonder how we would have felt if we could have known what was going to happen in the next twenty-four hours.

We were in bivouac that night, and before dawn the next morning we moved into our positions. I remember the scene so very well . . .

Our gun positions were in a huge cornfield on the forward slope of a hill. The stooks of corn, all ready for harvesting, provided ideal camouflage for the guns, and we dug ourselves in as best we could. My only protection consisted of a hole in the ground, about the height of a man, known as a "funk-hole", and very useful it proved to be, as we had no other cover.

Of course in those days all the units were horse-drawn, mechanisation being unheard of, and cavalry was still being employed on both sides.

The regiment consisted of four batteries of three eighteen-pounder guns and one 4,5 Howitzer battery, and all guns were horse-drawn. With each gun having eighteen horses to bring it into action, and various other horses required as outriders, there were some one hundred and fifty horses in each battery. Once the guns had been placed in position, all horses and drivers were withdrawn to the wagon lines a mile or so behind the battery.

As the light improved, I looked over the guns towards the enemy and could see in the far distance troop movement which was obviously German — my first sight of the enemy — but well out of range. The regiment had come into action with all four batteries in line facing the same direction. All was quiet as we waited for the Hun to make the first move, which he did at about 10 a.m., shelling our positions very accurately, until about 12 noon. During this time we had had about half-a-dozen guns knocked out and a number of casualties among the gun crews. Although the shelling had now almost ceased we were still getting a number of casualties, and couldn't understand it. We suddenly realised that they were caused by a sniper with a machine gun which had been installed in the church tower of the nearby village of Le Cateau. This enabled them to enfilade our batteries. Steps were taken to put him out of action, but by then we realised that the Germans had occupied the village.

I then noticed that our two flank batteries had swung back and were pointing at right angles to the original line of fire, so that the whole regiment formed an open square, reminiscent of the Napoleonic Wars. This indicated, even to a "rookie" like myself, that things were not going too well, and subsequent events proved that this was putting it mildly!

We then got orders to prepare for a cavalry attack — something unheard of in twentieth century warfare — which brought the Charge of the Light Brigade to mind. However, we prepared for the attack by setting all shrapnel ammunition at "Fuse O." This meant that the guns would fire at a very short range — about one thousand yards. Having made the necessary preparations we were then ordered to wait.

This episode of the war is something which I shall never forget. Suddenly over the horizon came the Uhlans — the elite German cavalry regiment. They came at full gallop, in close formation, their distinctive helmets shining in the brilliant sunshine and their lances at the ready. In spite of the tense situation I couldn't help thinking of the poem written about the Charge of the Light Brigade at Balaclava: "On, on, on rode the 600 . . ."

Well, on and on they came, this crack regiment of Prussian cavalry who won such fame in the Franco-Prussian war. They charged towards us, to what was tantamount to almost certain death. One could only admire this incredible display of courage.

When they reached a suitable distance the order came: "Open fire — gun fire", the latter meaning that all guns fired at maximum speed of six rounds per minute. The result of this was sheer pandemonium and devastation among the enemy. The poor devils never stood a chance and not one of them ever reached the guns. Riderless horses, bewildered and terrified, galloped all over the place. The survivors withdrew and, incredible as it may seem, launched a further attack a short time later with equally devastating results.

After this debacle all was quiet for a time, apart from the odd shell. Then the German infantry appeared. Their tactics were to open fire from 'a prone position and then move forward in short rushes. We dealt with them in the same way as the cavalry, but our fire was not as effective against the infantry who were able to take a certain amount of cover. They were gradually closing in on us. However, due to the support of our own infantry who had previously pulled back through our lines and occupied the high ground behind us, the enemy were being contained.

Nevertheless, it was pretty obvious that we were fighting a losing battle, and the situation was becoming more and more chaotic. No one appeared to know quite what to do, until at about 4 p.m. the order came: "Save the guns."

I had never seen anything like it. Teams of our horses appeared on the high ground behind us in order to remove the guns from the battery positions. Each gun needed two teams of six horses plus their complement of outriders. The regiment, having twenty-four guns and twenty-four ammunition wagons, meant that some three hundred horses would have to come under enemy fire in order to rescue the guns.

The moment the gun teams appeared on the high ground behind us the Hun artillery opened up. The devastation was absolutely ghastly. Silhouetted against the skyline the horses provided a perfect target of which the Hun took full advantage. Men and horses were just blown to pieces. After some time only one team consisting of four horses and a limber managed to reach one of the guns, limber up and drag it over the high ground behind us.

We were still in position, doing what we could, although as we were practically cut off by the Hun we realised our position was hopeless. Our colonel, adjutant and two battery commanders had been killed, and many of the men, and the place was a shambles. Then, to our intense relief down came the order: "Every man for himself — destroy the guns." Never was an order more willingly obeyed.

The procedure for destroying the guns was to put a round of ammunition down the muzzle, load the gun from the breach, and with a long lanyard fire the gun which then destroyed it. But there was no time for this. The German infantry were closing in fast, and in order to stop the guns being used against us, we decided to remove the breaches. I helped one of the gunners to take the breach off a gun I was near. A great strapping chap he was, called Gunner Major. With Major carrying the breach we started to "leg it" as fast as we could up the slope behind the guns. Bullets were splattering all round us. As we reached the top of the slope, Gunner Major stumbled and fell forward on his face. I leant over and spoke to him, but there was no reply. Blood was coming out of a wound in his back and I realised that he was dead. There was nothing more I could do for him, so I picked up the breach and continued to retreat over the high ground — with all speed.

Luckily the breach had a handle, but, even so, as it weighed about 25 lbs it was pretty hard going to run and carry it as well as my other equipment. Anyway, after running a short distance, to my great relief, I came across a French farmhouse. In the farmyard I spotted the inevitable cesspool, which every French farmhouse had in those days. This seemed to be the ideal place to dispose of the breach, so I flung it in, thinking that no Hun would ever find it there. I then had a quick look round the farmhouse hoping to find something to eat, as I was damned hungry, having had little or no food all day.

However, the farmer had obviously decided that retreat was the better part of valour, and the farmhouse was completely deserted. I then made off to the pre-arranged rendezvous and rejoined the remnants of the regiment and, to my joy, found my horse.

That was virtually the end of the 22nd Field Brigade. Completely exhausted both mentally and physically, we then started to move south, the only redeeming feature in that long night being the fact that the weather was fine and warm. The Germany cavalry kept harassing the column, and on that account we were only able to move short distances at a time.

Moving at only a walking pace, I kept dropping asleep and falling forward onto the horse's neck, which jerked me back into consciousness again. My face became quite sore with falling onto the horse's mane, and several times I nearly fell off altogether. I eventually evolved a plan to prevent this by tying the stirrups under the horse's tummy, which proved quite successful.

The question of food was now becoming pretty desperate. This was solved to some extent by the Commissariat Department which had dumped piles of cases containing bully, biscuits, jam and cheese as they retreated along the road. But, owing to the fact that we were being hounded by the Hun and kept on the move, we hadn't sufficient time to open the boxes.

It was one of the most hellish nights I have ever spent and I longed for daylight. With the dawn came some relief from harassment and we were able to get a move on. The roads were congested by thousands of French and Belgian civilian refugees who were also trying to escape from the common enemy.

As we passed through various villages and towns the population came out waving flags and shouting *Vive l'Angleterre*. At every opportunity they gave us coffee, bread and fruit. The latter nearly put me out of action altogether, as I developed a severe bout of diarrhoea, to add to all the other problems. Fortunately "my Mum", knowing I was susceptible to upset tummies, had provided me with a bottle of chlorodyne which saved the day.

This slow, deadly retreat continued, and the only encouraging thought was that we might end up in Gay Paree! At one point during the day we managed to cross the river Aisne, with our only surviving gun and four horses. We crossed at Soissons where the bridge was still intact. The retreat continued until we crossed the river Marne, and there we halted.

During this falling back period we were able to do some good with our rather pathetic 18-pounder gun and its depleted team of horses. German cavalry patrols were harassing the rearguard of which we formed part, and we were able to give them a damn good shelling from time to time, and inflict quite a bit of damage.

2

First battle of Ypres

About a week after the battle of Le Cateau and the subsequent retreat, the French under Marshal Foch put in an attack on our right flank. This halted the Germans who then began to fall back. So our visit to Paris had to be postponed and we began to prepare for an advance. This improved the morale of our troops, which had been at a pretty low ebb since Le Cateau. In those days, as I had not yet acquired the vices of drinking or smoking, and knew practically nothing about women, there was no distraction from our condition.

Orders now came to prepare for an advance. Sappers had thrown a pontoon bridge across the river Marne, as by now the enemy had destroyed all the main bridges. But the pontoon wasn't completed, in that it had no side rails. However, we were so anxious to get back and chivvy the Hun that we decided to take our gun across. At this juncture the Germans started shelling the bridge, and as the horses and gun were about half-way across a shell pitched into the river and threw up a great spout of water. This naturally terrified the horses, who sheered off the bridge, dragging the gun with them into the river. The gun sank and dragged the horses with it, so that the unfortunate animals were drowned. So it was that we lost our last remaining gun, and with it any chance that we might have had of pursuing the enemy in retreat.

Our immediate task now was to try and retrieve the gun and release the horses. We were just debating how on earth to do this, when a British N.C.O. came up to me and said he could help as he had been a diver in civvy street. Thanks to him we were able to release the horses, attach drag ropes to the gun and, with the help of the many infantrymen about, were able to drag the gun onto the bank. However, with no horses, and the gun possibly being useless, we were temporarily out of the war. It was quite heartbreaking to feel that after such a short period of action our unit had been practically wiped out.

After a suitable time of "mourning" we went to a reinforcement camp and were re-equipped, re-armed and re-mounted, and by then were rearing to go and have another crack at the Boche.

We were now advancing in a northerly direction and the Hun was making very little effort to stop us. As we passed through the many little villages the French people gave us an ecstatic welcome with as much food and as much cognac as they could muster. I remember one village specially where we bivouaced. The villagers crowded round us, telling us about the *sale Boche.* Apparently the local baker had been ordered to bake bread for the German troops. This he did and "to show their appreciation" they had then thrown him into the empty oven and closed the doors. Most of the women in the village had been raped, and we found one woman dead and naked in some bushes. Such is the tragedy of war, and even among disciplined troops these unpleasant incidents do occur.

One morning during our advance to the north we were temporarily halted by a German rearguard action. A number of Prussian officers had been captured and I got into conversation with them. The fact that they had been captured didn't stop them boasting — there was no doubt about the outcome of the war and they were going to win it. Their English at any rate was excellent.

While I was talking to them a stretcher with a body on it went past. The casualty was covered with a blanket, but I could just see the back of his head. At that moment I thought no more about it, and then it suddenly struck me, "I know the back of that head." I dashed after the stretcher, which by this time was in the casualty clearing station. I spoke to a doctor and said: "Have you seen a chap who looks just like me? He was brought in on a stretcher a few minutes ago."

The doctor said: "Good Lord yes, he's over there among that lot." I walked over and sure enough it was my twin brother, Vic, alive but unconscious. I asked the doctor what the trouble was, and he said they didn't know, but it was possible that he had been poisoned, as the Germans had been poisoning the wells.

I hung about for a bit, hoping that he would regain consciousness. We were likely to move into action at any moment, so I kept dodging between the battery and my brother. Eventually he came round, not knowing what was the matter with him, but convinced that he'd "had it." He asked me to take all his personal belongings — watch, ring, money etc., and send them back home. I tied them all in a handkerchief and went back to the battery.

It then occurred to me that as we were about to go into action, and that Vic would be evacuated to England, my chances of survival were a lot slimmer than his. So back I rushed and handed all the stuff back to him, and explained why. It turned out that he had a burst appendix and was very lucky not to have died of peritonitis. Anyway, that was the end of his war service in France.

Vic fully recovered and lived to fight in World War II where he escaped capture at Dunkirk. He is still going strong and living in Dorset.

As we advanced we spotted a German battery some distance away in the open, and immediately were ordered into action. We proceeded to shell them for about two hours — and blotted them out. We finally came up to the German position and were able to see how effective our fire had been. As we had been in a covered position we were at a great advantage and had very few casualties. I had never before seen the effect of our fire on a live target and the sight before us was really shattering. Guns and vehicles were smashed to pieces with many of the enemy dead. Among the latter was a German officer, who was wearing a very good pair of Zeiss field glasses round his neck. As I felt he had no further use for them I took them and had them for many years.

They proved very useful, but eventually they were stolen while

I was in India, so it was a case of *quid pro quo* — although I felt that I at least had earned them.

We continued to advance and the Germans continued to fall back until we reached the town of Ypres, where the Germans had taken up a strong position, forming a deep salient round the town itself, a position they held for many moons. We took up a position just outside Ypres near the Menin Gate and the Germans began to shell the town with heavy calibre guns. They kept up this bombardment until the town was virtually destroyed, including the lovely old Cloth Hall.

To give some idea of the calibre of the guns which the Germans were using to destroy Ypres, I was standing in the wagon lines where the horses were kept, and watching the shells pitching into Ypres. They were throwing up great clouds of dust and smoke, as buildings crumbled and fell. Suddenly, what we thought was a shell came towards us, pitched into the ground some yards away, but didn't explode. We were lying flat on our faces, expecting the thing to explode at any minute, but nothing happened. Eventually out of curiosity, we had it dug up, and discovered it was the complete base of a sixteen inch naval shell. This proved to be most useful as we converted it into an anvil for use by the farrier.

At this time the German Air Force began harassing us with machine-gun fire. As ack-ack guns were not in existence, and our own Air Force was being used mainly for reconnaissance work, we decided to try and provide some counter measures. We dug the trail of one of our 18-pounders into the ground to give it an almost perpendicular angle of fire. Using shrapnel we engaged a German plane without much effect, apart from killing one of our horses with the empty shell case which fell to the ground in our own lines, so we abandoned this form of counter-attack.

It was pretty obvious that we were in for a long spell of static warfare. The popular prediction that "it will all be over by Christmas" seemed to be turning into a pipe dream, and it was just as well that we didn't know what we were in for.

At that stage in the war we had practically no ammunition for the guns and were rationed to about four rounds per gun per day. This enabled us to keep a small reserve of ammo in case of an attack by the Germans. With the onset of the winter of 1914/15 our infantry were digging deeper trenches, and providing themselves with dugouts as some protection from the elements as well as the enemy. We as gunners were better off than the P.B.I. (poor bloody infantry) as we always had deep dugouts prepared at the gun position. The only time that we had to use the trenches was when we went up to the front line to do observation work. Once at the observation post we had a well-built dugout to live in.

As the static war developed in the Ypres salient, observation balloons became the "in thing." The Germans also adopted them and the sky became literally festooned with these stationary inflammable balloons. It became a sort of sporting event to try and shoot each other's balloons out of the sky. Ours were manned by men of the Observer Corps, who were equipped with parachutes for emergency landings — often needed.

One of these balloons was anchored to a special vehicle very near to our mess. One Sunday morning I was enjoying a well-earned beer when a chap from the Observer Corps came in and offered me a trip in his balloon as things were pretty quiet that day. I was interested to see what the enemy lines looked like, and was just about to leave when I was called to the telephone. I received orders to carry out an exercise, which prevented my balloon trip.

A brother officer enthusiastically took my place and up he went with the two Observer Corps chaps. These balloons were anchored to the ground by means of a steel hawser which in turn was connected to a winch, which was carried by a special vehicle. Once the men got into the basket the winch started working and the balloon ascended to a pre-determined height. We watched the balloon gaining height, and everything seemed to be all right, until we heard a gun fire, and the next thing we saw was that the cable holding the balloon had been severed by a million-to-one shot from the enemy guns. Fortunately, there was only a slight breeze as the balloon started to drift slowly towards the German lines. The occupants were seen to be struggling in their endeavours to get my brother officer into his parachute. They eventually managed to do this, and we watched as they descended in their "chutes." The two Observer Corps officers landed safely, but to my horror, my chap, unable through inexperience to control his parachute, drifted towards the Zilibeke Lake. Helplessly he was blown into the water, where the weight of his parachute held him down and he was drowned.

I couldn't help thinking what a narrow escape I had had. This was one of the many instances during my life in the army in which I escaped death by a short head.

By the end of 1914 most of the army was living underground like a lot of moles, and this life was to continue for the next three years. As a gunner my routine was as follows: two weeks in the front line in an O.P. (observation post), two weeks in the gunline with the guns and two weeks in the wagon line for a rest period.

The two weeks in the O.P. were spent keeping the enemy under observation. The O.P.s were right in the front line — only about 100 yards from the enemy. In consequence our movements were very restricted and during the day we were confined to the dugout. These were constructed strongly out of reinforced concrete or sandbags, with a lookout slit, and were built to accommodate four, or more in an emergency. They had been built by the sappers, who did a marvellous job as these dugouts could even withstand a direct hit.

The personnel in the O.P. consisted of two signallers, my batman and myself. We were in communication with the guns by field telephone, and could also communicate with brigade and divisional headquarters in the same manner. Our grub used to be brought up every night by way of the trenches, and pretty bloody it was too. We had facilities for making tea in the dugout on a paraffin stove.

In the early stages of the war this O.P. duty was boring as we were so limited with ammunition that there was very little to observe. After dark we used to emerge mole-like from our little holes and take a bit of exercise, although there was always the risk of snipers. "Very" lights were fired constantly by us and the enemy, and any movement would attract a sniper's bullet. Drinking water was brought up with the rations, but washing water was often taken from a shellhole, providing it was free of dead bodies. The whole front line area was littered with dead, and it was often impossible to remove them.

Whenever possible they were buried *in situ* and if the opportunity arose they were re-buried later.

One of the worst features of trench warfare was trying to keep clean. It was practically impossible to keep free of body lice as we couldn't change our clothes for two weeks at a time, and sometimes for as long as two months. We had to burn the seams of our clothes with a candle to destroy the eggs. Our flannel shirts and sheepskin jackets were ideal breeding grounds for those filthy creatures. My dear old Mum, in concern for my welfare, sent me some lovely fleece-lined vests and long underpants. Of course, every louse in France made a bee-line for me!

The second two weeks in a normal tour of duty were in the wagon lines, about five miles back from the front, and usually near a village where we would be billeted. There, for two blissful weeks, we could get hot baths, beds and decent grub.

One billet I remember particularly well was the farmhouse of Mme de Tournai at Dranoutre, whose husband was fighting with the French forces at Verdun. She was a charming, motherly person who was struggling to keep the farm going on her own. She looked after me like a son, and what a treat it was to have some home cooking. She tried several times to bring my early morning tea, much to my batman's disapproval. My batman — a huge red-headed Irishman called Murphy — took the tray from her at the bedroom door and took upon himself the role of a Victorian chaperone, saying with a broad Irish brogue: "It's not right for her to come in here, Sir, it's my job."

I became quite interested in the farm and did what I could to help Madame. Late one night I was wakened by frantic banging on my bedroom door and Madame de Tournai's agitated voice calling: *La vache, la vache, malade, malade, venez vite!* or words to that effect.

I dressed hurriedly and went to the cowshed where one of the cows seemed to be having some difficulty in delivering her calf. Madame had managed to get a rope round the little fellow and she asked my batman and me to pull on the rope in order to assist the delivery. With much moaning from the cow and sweat on our part we managed to deliver a sturdy little calf. I now rather fancied myself as a cowhand, and took a great interest in the little fellow's progress.

While billeted in Dranoutre I was attached to Brigade Head-quarters. Also attached to the Brigade was a French officer called Major Hennin, who acted as our interpreter. He and I became very friendly and as we had time on our hands he offered to teach me French by the Berlitz method. In consequence my French improved considerably and this was invaluable during the next three years in France. On one occasion old Hennin was going on leave to Paris, and asked if there was anything he could bring me as a present. I said, "Yes thanks, I really don't mind if it's a blonde or a brunette." To which he replied, in all seriousness: *Ce n'est pas possible.*

However, it transpired that Major Hennin was a manufacturing jeweller in civilian life, and the present that he did bring me was a set of beautiful gold-plated silver teaspoons. On the handle of each was embossed the figure of Britannia stepping out of a boat with the words *Entente Cordiale.* I still have them and they are one of my most treasured possessions.

I nearly lost them in World War II when my mother was looking after them in London. Her house got a direct hit from a doodle-bug and was completely destroyed. Luckily my mother had moved to the country the day before, and my teaspoons and other valuables were rescued the following day by my twin brother before the looters got busy.

While in the Ypres area I stayed in a couple more pleasant billets. One of these was with a mother and daughter, the latter being a sweet little girl of about seventeen. On one occasion some of the lads and myself decided to go to the local "pub", or *estaminet* as they were called in France. Up to that stage in my life I had been a strict teetotaller, and had promised my mother that I would keep off the stuff which, according to her, had been my father's downfall. Having got to the pub the other chaps persuaded me that champagne was non-alcoholic. In my youth and innocence I was fool enough to believe them, but after the first couple of bottles began to realise that I wasn't drinking lemonade! On the way back home I found difficulty in staying on the right course, but eventually made it back to the billet. I flopped on my bed fully clothed and wearing a very posh pair of fleece-lined rubber knee boots, which were heavily coated with Flanders mud. After a while I heard voices, French, female and very agitated. In my muzzy state I realised that their concern was for my boots, or rather for their clean bed linen which was being ruined by the mud on them. It was the mother and daughter of the house who then proceeded to try to remove my boots. Of course, to get them off in my condition was practically impossible as the wearer was incapable of giving any assistance. Eventually they abandoned the attempt and I was left in peace to wake up next morning, still wearing my boots.

On my way to breakfast in the mess I was met by a very disgruntled Madame, and I couldn't blame her. Diplomatic relations were restored after I had apologised and offered to pay for any damage caused.

While on the subject of billets, I was once billeted with another mother and daughter in the same area of Belgium. This daughter was also about seventeen and very pretty. She seemed very anxious to bring my early morning tea, much to old Murphy's disgust. He used to waylay her at my bedroom door and take the tray, as at the previous billet. However, on one occasion, she managed to give Murphy the slip and appeared with the tray at my bedside. She sat on the edge of my bed and we "parleyed" a bit of French. Suddenly, without any warning she hopped into bed with me. I was absolutely terrified, jumped out of bed and ran like a scalded cat! I returned a short time later to discover that mademoiselle had departed.

To show how naive I was, I told the chaps in the mess about my "terrifying experience." They said: "You bloody fool! Why did you waste an opportunity like that? Next time it happens send for one of us!" However, unfortunately, this particular kind of hospitality wasn't forthcoming again, and I was treated with the scorn that I deserved.

I realise that from a present day point of view this sounds perfectly ludicrous, but those were the days when virginity in the young of both sexes was the norm, rather than the exception.

I have mentioned these little incidents to show the brighter side of life in the trenches, and that my three years in World War I weren't all mud, blood and body lice.

3

From rats to royalty

During my time in the Ypres Salient we were to suffer the first German gas attack. I remember it so clearly. We were in action but not doing much firing, although there was heavy fighting on the northwest part of the Salient. I noticed what I thought was a rather heavy morning mist close to the ground about a mile away. It was a strange yellowish colour, and appeared to be drifting towards us. I gave it no further thought until a steady stream of British infantrymen started to appear behind the guns. I went to question them and saw that they were in batches of three, the men on either side supporting what turned out to be a gas casualty.

These poor devils seemed to be suffocating with their tongues swollen to three or four times their normal size and sticking out of their mouths. I questioned the non-casualties and they told me that the Germans had launched this gas attack, and had taken them completely by surprise with no gas masks or protection of any kind. As a result of this our line had given way on a four-mile front. Particularly affected were the French colonial troops, who were panic stricken and completely demoralised by this new horror. Luckily the Canadian troops were being moved up to the line and were pushed into the breach with little or no preparation. They closed the gap and saved the day.

I then saw that the yellow cloud — which by this time I realised was gas — was still moving towards us, slowly but surely. Something had to be done if the battery was going to be saved, but what?

I dashed over to the Quarterbloke's Store, which was located in a farmhouse nearby, and asked him if we had any anti-gas appliances, telling him about the casualties I had just seen. He replied: "I don't know, Sir, but some stuff came up in boxes the other day. Haven't had a chance to open them yet." On opening the boxes we discovered that they contained masses of gauze masks of the type worn in operating theatres. We frantically rushed the boxes to behind the battery position, called the men to collect their masks and read the instructions, which were as follows: "The pad is impregnated with a chemical which is activated by moistening with water. If no water is available you should urinate on it."

I was keeping an eye on the cloud of gas and now noticed that it had come to within 500 yards of the battery, and wondered just how effective our "Heath Robinson" masks were going to be.

Having obeyed the instructions about the masks as best we could, and put them round our necks, all we could do was wait. Then nothing short of a miracle happened. The wind changed. As we watched in amazement the cloud rolled back right onto the German lines and halted the enemy advance.

After many further engagements, such as Hill 60, Messines Ridge, and so on, we were moved down to Bray-sur-Somme, where we were to take part in the first battle of the Somme.

On our way down to the Somme to relieve the French at Bray, we bivouacked at a small village called Corbé on the bank of the river Ancre. As we were likely to be there for the night, some of the chaps and I decided to nip across the river and see what Corbé had to offer by way of entertainment. We crossed over the bridge about a mile down the river and found the local estaminet which was opposite the cathedral. It was a nice little pub and we had an effusive reception from Monsieur le patron. As I was still not hooked on hard tack it was decided to order champagne, which was available all over France and very reasonably priced. We ordered a magnum of Veuve Cliquot between the four of us and, having knocked that back, followed it with three more!

At this stage I decided to go outside and get a breath of fresh air, and once on my feet I began to feel old widow Cliquot's mixture taking effect. I sat down on a bench outside facing the cathedral, and started to count the stones in the cathedral wall, finding that this reduced my dizzy feeling. Eventually I went back into the pub and found that the proprietor was standing us another bottle. By this time it was late afternoon and I thought it was about time to get back to the battery in case orders came for us to move. So as the senior subaltern I said: "Come on chaps, let's get weaving," and I'm afraid that "weave" was the operative word.

On reaching the river bank by a footpath, we found that the bridge we had crossed earlier in the day was a mile upstream, but immediately in front of us was a footbridge used by the local inhabitants. It had no side rails and was very narrow and rickety.

The other three who carried their liquor better than I did, said: "Come on, let's get across here." I replied that I couldn't possibly get across that bridge in my present state. Well, off the other three fellows went, and left me to get back as best I could. Eventually I decided to sit astride the bridge and worked my way over by using my hands, while the other chaps jeered from the opposite bank. Anyway, I made it to the other side, sweating like the proverbial *cochon*.

We arrived back at the battery where I was met by my batman. "Here you are Sir, this is where you're gonna sleep." My "bedchamber" was a 'paulin thrown over the pole of the limber which was attached to the gun. I was in no condition to protest, and in any case there was nothing better to be had, so I crept in under the 'paulin and went to sleep. In that condition I think I could have slept on a clothesline.

The alarm was sounded at the ungodly hour of 4 a.m. and roused me out of my drunken stupor. It had rained during the night and I was wet through, frozen, and had the most ghastly hangover. The frightful cup of tea brought by my batman was the one bright spot.

We were ordered to move within the hour. I had no change of

clothing, so still soaking wet, I just managed to mount my horse, but had considerable difficulty in remaining "on board." The battery was assembled and we moved off. After about an hour we reached the place where we were to take up our positions to support the French, and by this time I was feeling a good deal better.

The French were already in action at Bray and we relieved them. They removed their *soixante-quinze* guns and we put ours into their emplacements, which had been well constructed. That night, having settled in as well as we could, I went to sleep in my dugout, fully clothed except for my boots. During the night I was woken by a ghastly pain in my right foot. By the light of my torch I saw a giant rat nibbling my big toe. I heaved a boot at him and he disappeared, but from then on I wore my boots at night.

Next morning when I went to inspect the guns I found the troops in a great state of agitation on account of these bloody great rats. They really were as big as cats and no-one had had any sleep. The whole place was infested with them. We discovered that the French infantry had been burying their dead in the parados of the trenches, and this had drawn an army of rats who had been living on human flesh. It was obvious that something had to be done about it. We then discovered that owing to their eating habits they had developed a terrific thirst, and as a result rat hunting became a nightly sport with the gun crews. They used to fill canvas buckets with water, and armed with sticks would wait for the thirsty rats to come up and drink. Each morning at inspection the gun crews would parade their dead rats in order of size, and the crew who had killed the most would get an extra tot of rum.

These rats became so bold that one actually attacked me like a dog when I tried to kill it by jumping on it, and I was forced to retreat as I was unarmed at the time. When a colony of rats decided to move nothing would stop them.

Early one morning I went into Bray-sur-Somme, through which a convoy had passed during the night. At the same time a colony of rats had crossed the road and the whole area was a mass of squashed rats, a revolting sight. I never saw rats in such numbers anywhere else in France or Belgium.

One day, when I was up in the O.P., one of the infantry commanders came in. He pointed out a road running at right angles to our infantry trenches. The commander said that every night the old Boche was coming up with his ammo wagons and rations, and as they were horse-drawn they made quite a din on the cobblestones. He suggested that we should give them a walloping one night. I agreed but pointed out that this would mean bringing up a gun and putting it in the trenches, as owing to the flat trajectory of the 18-pounder we couldn't reach the target from our position.

It was a bold and exciting plan. The C.O. and I did a recce that night in order to decide on the route by which to bring up the gun. We would need about twenty-four men to man the drag-ropes and some solid duckboards to bridge the trenches which would have to be crossed. The gun had to be accurately positioned in relation to the road we were going to shell as it wasn't possible to do a pre-determined shoot without giving the game away.

All necessary preparations were then made and, on the first suitable dark night, with much sweating and heaving, and with the enemy only about three hundred yards away, we managed to get the gun into position. The trickiest part was when we actually got near the trenches and the Hun kept firing Very lights. If they had spotted us we wouldn't have had a hope in hell. However, we finally got the gun into the trench and covered it with camouflaged netting.

The gun was then left for a week and during that time we took up about a hundred rounds of ammo. On a given night, acting on info from the infantry, the gun crew and I moved up to the gun site. We prepared the ammo and waited. After an hour or so we could hear in the distance the rumble of the approaching German wagons. This gradually grew louder as the wagons came closer and and when it ceased we knew that they had reached the unloading point. We then opened gun-fire with mixed ammo — shrapnel and high explosive. There was great activity from the German lines with machine-gun fire, but they hadn't actually located us. We'd got off about eighty rounds when a German trench mortar shell fell too damn close for our comfort, followed by several others.

This was our congé, so we camouflaged the gun and "legged it." I spent the night in the O.P. and at the crack of dawn I turned my binoculars onto the area which we had shelled. Although I say it myself, we had done a pretty good job. My C.O., who joined me, said jokingly: "Damn good show Hodgson, I'll see you get the V.C. for this."

After this little effort we left the gun where it was for about a fortnight with instructions that no-one was to go near it. Any possibility of repeating the exercise was now futile as the element of surprise had been lost.

The C.O. was rather against bringing the gun out again if it meant incurring any casualties, now that the Germans were on the alert. However, we eventually decided to remove the gun at the infantry's request as they said it was drawing a lot of fire from the enemy. So we repeated the exercise in reverse, with no casualties, due to the fact, I think, that the Boche never accurately located the gun.

During our period on the Somme we were turned into Corps Artillery. We were detached from our brigade and became a sort of mobile unit, and were under orders of Corps H.Q. We were liable to be moved to any part of the Corps front as needed. On one occasion we were called in to support the South African forces at Delville Wood.

This battle became one of the epics of World War I and the South Africans suffered tremendous losses. By a strange coincidence when I came to South Africa some thirty years later, and became secretary of the 1820 Settlers' Association, my chairman was a man called Jack Shave, who had been severely wounded at Delville Wood.

At about this time, having served for two years in the line, the powers that be saw fit to pull us out and send us to a place called St. Pol for a comparative "rest." It was a delightful little place, and the local château was used as our officers' mess. The Marquis and his family were still in residence and were very friendly towards us. We were formed into a school of gunnery and I became one of the instructors, in the practical and theoretical sides of gunnery.

Edward, Prince of Wales (later to become the Duke of Windsor) and his aide-de-camp Battenberg (later to become Earl Mountbatten of Burma) joined the school and became my pupils. Edward was then a captain in one of the Guards regiments — I think it was the Grenadiers. Although only about eighteen at the time, he was already quite a lad with the girls and enjoyed his drinks.

The largest reception room in the château had been allocated as the officers' mess dining room. It had the most magnificent chandeliers, made of cut glass. One evening we had a guest night and the Prince distinguished himself by getting rather "tiddly" and standing on a table downing a succession of drinks and throwing the empty glasses at the chandeliers. The Marquis, who wasn't present at the time, "was not amused" and next morning there was quite a hoo-haa. However, the matter was amicably settled when H.R.H. offered to pay for the damage.

I remember being present when the Marquis, his wife and two daughters were presented to the Prince, and how nervous he was — quite understandable in the circumstances, I suppose. Part of the Prince's "equipment" at St. Pol were two Rolls Royce cars, which he allowed us to use when he didn't require them. We used to go into the nearby town of Béthune where there was an officer's shop.

Prince Edward's greatest wish was to get up to the front line where his regiment was in action, but he was constantly frustrated by officialdom which was concerned for his safety. Wherever he went he was watched and his movements reported to H.Q. I believe that he did eventually manage to get up to the line for a short time, before being brought back to comparative safety. On one occasion a report came through that he had been seen going into a local hotel with a couple of mademoiselles. However, on that occasion he was given a bit of rope.

H.R.H. and Mountbatten used to attend my classes on gunnery, and appeared to be reasonably interested. During one lecture I thought that the Prince seemed to be particularly interested. He hardly looked up from the barrack room table at which he was sitting, and appeared to be taking copious notes throughout the lecture.

When the lecture was finished and the class dismissed, I walked to where he had been sitting to see if there was any evidence of what he had been writing. To my utter amazement and amusement, I found that he had not been writing at all. He had in fact been cutting into the table with a pen knife, and this is what he had written:

> "I love the girls who do,
> I love the girls who don't,
> I love the girl who says she will,
> And then you find she won't.
> But, of all the girls that I love best,
> And I think you'll say I'm right,
> Is the girl who says she never does,
> But looks as though she might!"

This little verse isn't an original Royal masterpiece as I thought, nor is it quite what it appears to imply. I believe it is in fact called "An ode to a kiss." I was so "tickled" by this literary effort that I memorised it, and there was a sequel to the incident some five years later. I was stationed at a place called Weedon in Northants, undergoing a two-year course as a riding instructor. We were privileged to be invited to hunt with some of the best known fox hunting packs in England, the Pytchley, Quorn, Grafton, North Warwick, and so on. The Prince of Wales was a very keen horseman and often used to hunt with these packs.

On one occasion the Pytchley was meeting quite close to Weedon, but the hunt had to be abandoned because of a heavy mist. It was decided to invite members of the hunt, including the Prince, back to Weedon to ride the steeple-chase course.

After a quick one in the mess we were paraded to be formally introduced to the Prince. When it came to my turn we shook hands and as he looked at me he said: "I know your face. Haven't we met before?" I replied: "Yes Sir, St. Pol Gunnery School, 1916."

"Ah yes, I remember," he said, and as he moved on to the next person I said: "I love the girls who do . . ." He turned back and gave a loud chuckle. Apparently he had not forgotten.

4

Mustard gas and mustard baths

The idyllic conditions of St. Pol didn't last very long, and we were ordered to go up to relieve the French at the Yser Canal in Belgium. There we resumed our mole-like life once more.

Immediately on arrival the C.O. said to me: "Hodgson, I'd like you to go up and relieve that bloody Froggy in the O.P."

So off I went, reaching the O.P. by means of the communication trenches. The trenches were well constructed and in immaculate condition, which rather indicated that very little fighting had been going on. I got to the O.P. to be met by a very pleasant captain in the French artillery. We went inside and it was absolutely magnificent. Quite spacious, with proper beds and furniture, two rooms, and the whole place decorated with wall-paper — and all this only fifty yards from the Hun lines!

When I recovered from the surprise I said to him: "Don't you ever do any fighting here?" To which he replied that they had a sort of agreement with the Germans that they wouldn't attack unless they did. As a result of this they had had very few casualties and very little fighting in the last two years. It seemed to me a sensible idea.

The French captain and I then set about doing the handing and taking over, and he explained about the lines of fire and other technicalities. I suggested that we fired on some of the targets, but he wouldn't hear of it, appearing to be very reluctant to "disturb" the enemy!

The captain suggested that we have a drink, which I thought was an excellent idea. He then made the most startling suggestion of the day. He said: "Would you like to take over my girl-friend?"

I said: "What? Girl-friend — up here?"

"Yes," he said.

He then went on to explain that as there had been so little fighting in the area they had naturally looked to their comfort.

I said, "Well, let's have a look at her." Whereupon he called a name — something like Fifi — and out of the adjacent room there emerged a most attractive girl. We were introduced and exchanged a few pleasantries in French, after which she withdrew, and the captain asked me what I thought. I replied that I thought it would be an excellent idea, but didn't know how my C.O. would react to it, and I would have to ask him. After all, it was rather an unusual situation — in the British Army in any case.

So back I went to the guns and told the C.O. what had happened. He nearly had a stroke. "Good heavens man, you can't do a thing like that — at least not in the trenches! We're at war. Go back and tell that bloody Froggy that this sort of thing doesn't go on in the British Army."

I felt his attitude was a bit "dog in the manger-ish," but there was nothing more to be done, so back I went to the O.P. and most reluctantly turned down the captain's attractive offer. The gallant captain and his girl-friend then moved out and I moved in *tout seul.*

Incidentally, the location of our battery was rather unique, in that we were the battery on the extreme left of the whole of the western front. In fact, our No. 6 gun was almost on the beach. We used to watch the Hun infantry coming down early in the morning for a bathe, and would fire a couple of shells in their direction and watch them scuttling back to their trenches.

At this stage the Boche was in control of Ostend, and would shell the whole coastline with naval guns. We would watch these high velocity naval shells pitch into the sand-dunes and then skid along the sand like torpedos. More often than not they didn't explode, so that the whole coastline was littered with unexploded shells.

One of our many problems at this position was sickness among the horses. A number died of what we thought was colic — a common disease among horses. However, when the vet did an autopsy on one of the victims it was discovered that in eating their hay they had picked up a certain amount of beach sand. This had formed into a hard ball in the intestine. Owing to a deficiency in their diet they used to eat each other's tails if they got the opportunity, so we had to short halter them fore and aft.

At this stage in the war the intention was to try and capture Ostend from the sea, attacking from the right and left flanks and frontal. To this end we were practising landing and re-embarking guns, horses and men from flat-bottomed landing craft. It was quite a job and I couldn't see much future in it under enemy fire.

However, fate stepped in. In order for our three-pronged attack to succeed it was necessary for the French on the right flank to capture Holdhurst Forest. Fortunately, or unfortunately, their attack failed and the whole project was abandoned.

The powers that be then decided to withdraw a large number of troops that had been concentrated for the Ostend attack, but my battery was left in its original position near Oost Dunikerke.

It was then that we had our first mustard gas attack. One night the Germans opened up on us as they normally did. There was a crossroad very near our battery position and I think that was really their target, trying to disrupt communications. On this particular night we thought they were firing a lot of dud shells, as they didn't appear to explode, but landed with a noise rather like that of pulling a cork from a bottle.

The shelling went on all night, and in the morning I got up and did a chukka round the battery position and then noticed a number of shallow shell holes. Round the rim of the shell hole there was a sort of treacly substance, a brownish colour. I had no idea what it was, so I rang up Divisional H.Q. and they sent up a couple of chemical experts. I took them to one of the shell holes and one of them said: "Good heavens, that's mustard gas; you're damn lucky. The temperature is so low that the gas hasn't evaporated."

We were then told to treat all the adjacent shell holes with chloride of lime.

These two chaps then took specimens of the shells to be analysed. We invited them to stay for lunch — such as it was — and during the meal one of them complained of a burning sensation in his side. Apparently he had put one of the pieces of shell in his pocket and hadn't protected it properly, and the heat of his body had activated it. He explained that this substance, if in contact with the skin, would cause a most frightful suppurating sore which was very difficult to heal. Although these chaps were "experts" they really only knew it in theory, and this was the first practical experience they had had of the beastly stuff. They soon legged it back to H.Q. and we got busy taking the necessary precautions for our men and ourselves.

The Hun continued with this mustard gas shelling and caught one of the withdrawing columns on the main road with their pants down, and there were many thousands of gas casualties in consequence.

About this time a young officer joined us. In civilian life he had been a Burberry salesman. I asked him if he had had any training in gas warfare. He said he had been taught all about it in England, but had had no practical experience. I said: "Well, you'll get plenty here, as the Hun gases us practically all the time, specially at night."

That night, after a sumptuous dinner of bully and biscuits, the old Hun opened up with his gas shells, and I said to "Burberry": "Now you can show me what you know about gas."

We had to do a tour of inspection to see that the men were all alert and wearing their gas masks. The entrance to the dug-out was protected by two chemically-impregnated blankets, to prevent gas getting inside. I told "Burberry" to put on his mask and we stepped in between the blanket curtains. Before lifting the second one I checked up on my assistant to see that his mask was in order. Everything seemed to be all right, and as we stepped outside the Hun was really going at it "hammer and tongs," and shells were falling pretty close. One shell in particular pitched about fifteen yards away. I looked at "Burberry" and his gas mask had blown up into a great balloon, indicating that it wasn't properly adjusted. I dragged him back into the dug-out and asked him if he thought he had breathed in any gas. He seemed to think he was all right, so after a couple more trials with the mask we went out again to face the music. We had a chukka round the battery, all seemed to be well and the men were on the alert, cheerful and wearing their masks. On the way back to the dug-out we called in on the C.O. to make my report. I regret to say he was rather tight, half-asleep and not wearing his mask. We managed to get him into it and went back to the dug-out, which was also the mess.

The next morning young "Burberry" came to me and said he was feeling very ill. I said he'd probably inhaled some of the gas and, as it was too risky to take a chance, sent him up to the casualty clearing station. The next thing we heard was that he'd been evacuated back to England as a gas casualty. The poor blighter's time in the front line had been short and exceedingly sharp.

About three months later we were still in the same position on the Yser Canal, when young "Burberry" re-appeared for duty. I said: "You don't look at all well. Are you fit for duty?"

He said: "I've had a hell of a time. The small quantity of gas I inhaled has caused me to lose most of my hair, my teeth and I've also got a lung condition."

So I asked him: "What on earth possessed you to come back here?"

"I felt that I must do my bit."

I replied: "I think you've more than done that already."

I kept my eye on him for a few days and noticed that he seemed very distressed when wearing his respirator. He was obviously far from well, and eventually I persuaded him to report sick.

So off he went to the M.O. and they sent him back to England. He was one of the many courageous young chaps, who were determined to fight, no matter what the cost.

The ruddy Hun kept up this gas attack practically the whole time that we were on the Yser Canal. We had to wear our respirators constantly — almost day and night. They were the type that had a clip on the nose, with a tube going into the mouth, leading to a container which you carried in a haversack on your chest. After weeks of wearing this ruddy respirator our noses got terribly sore and we developed blisters which turned into hard callouses — just one of the many things that added to the comfort of trench warfare!

Life on the Yser Canal did have its brighter moments. Periodically, we went down to the wagon line where the horses and ammunition wagons were kept. Nearby was Oost Dunikerke which had a nice little watering hole called the Hotel Turlinque. There we could get decent grub, a clean bed and a bath. In spite of being shelled the patron had kept going and how grateful we were to him. However, the real *pièce de résistance* was when we could get down to La Panne on the Belgian coast. In peacetime it had been a popular seaside resort, and during the war military authorities established an enormous hopsital there. As there were about five hundred nurses of all nationalities working there, this provided us with a bit of relief, so that La Panne became the Mecca of every soldier within miles. The bathing was superb, with white sandy beaches where one could walk out into clear water for about half a mile without getting out of depth.

Attached to the hospital were places where one could have various kinds of baths. This was a marvellous way of getting clean and de-loused.

One day I decided to try a mustard bath. This section was run by an old French woman. The procedure was that you had an ordinary bath first. After that the French woman painted you all over with a mustard paste. You were then put into a hot cabinet which baked the mustard hard onto your skin. Next came another hot bath when you were scrubbed to get rid of the mustard. That completed, you were then allowed to have an ordinary bath "under your own steam." While this was going on your clothes were taken away and fumigated, killing all the lice and their eggs which had been acquired in the trenches. The sheer joy of feeling clean at last was quite indescribable. It did wonders for one's morale and we went back to the trenches feeling that we could take on the whole Hun army.

5

Passchendaele — mud, blood and body lice

As I had been in France since the outbreak of war, the powers that be decided to give me some leave. My C.O. suddenly said that I could push off the next day, on ten days leave to the U.K.

So the next morning I packed up my few belongings and got a lift by lorry to the nearest station. I caught a train to Paris and on arrival at the Gare du Nord we found ourselves in the middle of an air raid by Zeppelins. I decided that, if I were going to be killed, it certainly wouldn't be while going on leave, and in a train! That would be far too ignominious. So with others, I jumped out of the carriage and took cover under a railway truck filled with road metal, which provided good solid cover. There was chaos and pandemonium in the huge station while the raid lasted, but fortunately it was over quickly, and we continued our train journey to Le Havre. There we boarded a cross channel steamer and, in lifejackets and packed like sardines, we sailed for England.

All went well until we were about midway across the channel. It was a typical English summer day — cold and grey with a sea mist -- but fortunately the sea was calm. My thoughts were of England, peace, and generally getting away from it all when suddenly the alarm bell rang and a voice over the loud hailer shouted: "Enemy submarine sighted on the starboard bow."

There was a general feeling of apprehension, but no panic. The traditional British bulldog spirit came to the fore, and the hundreds of men who packed the decks just waited quietly, feeling like a lot of sitting ducks, for whatever fate had in store. At any moment we expected to feel the impact of a torpedo, and all at once the English coast seemed terribly far away.

Then came the order: "Stand down." And it subsquently transpired that the object the lookout had taken to be the submarine periscope was, in fact, an empty bottle of John Haig floating on the water some distance away.

The relief was terrific, and much ribald laughter ensued with many coarse and derogatory remarks at the expense of the Navy.

We eventually disembarked at Dover and I made my way via London to my mother's house near Epsom. There was a happy family reunion as her eldest of three soldier sons arrived home out of the blue.

Everyone in London seemed to be in uniform, and it was a case of an "eat, drink and be merry, for tomorrow we die." sort of attitude. The first day or so I spent getting cleaned up and de-loused. I was still acting as host to a certain number of lice and their eggs, much to my mother's disgust! Having left France in a hurry I hadn't been able to get rid of them before leaving.

One evening my twin brother and I took my mother out to dinner in the West End. We were walking up Regent Street when I was accosted by a rather flashy girl.

She said: "Have you got the time?"

To which I replied: "Yes, but not the inclination!" I rejoined my mother, who asked in all innocence: "Why don't you introduce me to your friend?"

On another occasion my two brothers and I went up to town for a bit of a binge. On our arrival at Victoria Station the air raid siren sounded and we were all ordered to take cover. We resisted but were eventually forced down into an Underground station, and what a sight it was. Hundreds of people apparently were living down there to escape the Zeppelin raids. I didn't think much of this as a way of spending my leave, and was glad when we resurfaced and were able to go off to our dinner and show. When we came out of the theatre my twin brother returned to his base at Deepcut, and Les, my youngest brother was spending the night in London — luckily for him. When I tried to get home to Epsom I discovered that all transport had been disrupted by the raid, and it was quite impossible to get a train, bus or taxi. There was no choice but to walk. This I did and arrived at my mother's house at 3 a.m. having walked ten miles.

Having reached home the next problem was to try and get in. After hammering on the front door for some time, an upstairs window was thrown up, and my mother's face appeared.

"Who's there?" my mother's haughty voice boomed out.

"It's me — Clarry," I called up from below.

Mother replied in the same icy tone, "Any what do you mean by coming home at this time of the night? I suggest you find some other place to sleep." Before I could reply, BANG went the window.

I thought, "this is a fine reception for a returning warrior" and continued to bang on the door.

After a considerable time the door was opened and mother appeared. Before she could say anything I told her what had happened and that I hadn't been on an all night orgy as she had thought. With tears and apologies I was admitted, and later that morning was even given breakfast in bed!

The rest of my leave seemed to be spent being led around like a performing bear, being introduced to all my mother's friends and relations. My mother was not much given to sentiment but was an extremely courageous woman. At one time her husband and three sons were all fighting in France, and to the world at large she never batted an eyelid. The nearest to tears that I ever saw her was on the day I went back to France. She came with me to Victoria and we walked together arm-in-arm down the platform. I felt that there was no prouder mother in all England, and I think we both wondered if it would be our last "goodbye."

Shortly after returning to the Yser Canal, the C.O. told me that I was to be posted to a new unit, at Passchendaele, the idea being to send officers with war experience to help the new units coming from England.

En route to Passchendaele I called in at the officer's club at Amiens for a meal and a drink. On coming out of the club later

I was accosted by a French girl who had apparently been reduced to prostitution as her husband was with the French troops at Verdun, who were under siege.

I accompanied her back to her rather squalid little flat, but had no inclination to have any relations with her. In fact the whole business was repugnant to me. We just had a drink and a chat and I was so sorry for the poor girl that on leaving I gave her five hundred francs which I had just drawn from the field cashier. This was the equivalent of about twenty-five pounds in those days. She'd obviously never had so much for doing so little and she burst into tears of gratitude and joy. For my part I felt that I had made a small contribution to the "Entente Cordiale!"

I subsequently joined one of the new divisions and the battery went up to the line and occupied a position on the Broodseinde Ridge overlooking Passchendaele Ridge. We were destined to take part in what was to become one of the bloodiest battles of World War I — if not THE bloodiest. From statistics I've read since, there were three hundred and fifty thousand casualties, killed and wounded, at Passchendaele. Our guns at Broodseinde Ridge were well dug in and the sappers had built an almost impregnable dug-out for officers, and a larger one of the same type for the men.

On my first morning at Broodseinde I went up to the O.P. from where there was an excellent view of the notorious Passchendaele Ridge. The O.P. was well protected and accommodated my batman and myself as well as two signallers.

Day and night firing from both sides never ceased and the whole area was one mass of shell holes and dead bodies. It was the nearest thing to Hell that one could imagine.

My major was a Territorial chap called Bell, who in civvy street was a stockbroker in Liverpool. One day he said to me: "Clarry, I've had enough of this — I'm going to get a Blighty One." The word "Blighty," by the way, was a corruption of the Hindustani word for England, which was Vilait. The British Tommy corrupted it to "Blighty." By "getting a Blighty One" we meant getting wounded badly enough to be evacuated back to England.

I told him he hadn't seen anything yet, as he'd only been in

France a few weeks, and asked him how he proposed to get the "Blighty One." He said he would go outside when the next shelling started. I should mention here that the Germans had a technique in which they concentrated all their artillery fire on one specified area. We used to call this shell storming.

On this particular morning they opened up and the major said: "I'm going out now and I'll probably get a Blighty One." I said, "All right, I'm coming with you; I think I'm more qualified for a Blighty One than you are!"

We went out to the guns that were firing, and German shells were falling all over the place. Suddenly the major pitched forward onto his face. We dragged him into the nearest dug-out and got him on to a stretcher. He was still unconscious as we stripped his clothes off.

He was wearing two sheepskin jackets which probably saved his life. Eventually the doctor came and found a huge bruise in the middle of Bell's back, caused by a big piece of shell which had knocked him out Luckily the piece of shell had hit him flatways on, otherwise he would certainly have been a dead man. When he came round and we told him what had happened he said: "I'm not going to try and get another Blighty One — that was too damn close."

I said: "Yes, if your number's on it you'll get it."

The very next day the major and I were going round the guns. The usual shelling was going on, and presently a shell burst fairly close. We both dived onto the ground to avoid it, but he got a piece through his arm which caused rather a nasty wound. So the major got his Blighty One after all. He was subsequently evacuated to England and never came back to France.

The Passchendaele offensive was commanded by General Haig. He appeared to be determined to capture Passchendaele Ridge at whatever cost. An attack was launched supported by tanks. This was one of the first tank attacks in military history. I was up at the O.P. at the time and many tanks were knocked out or conked out, as the tanks in those days were not of a very high standard, and eventually this attack failed. The fact that the guns got so hot that the gunners were able to light their cigarettes from the breach of the gun will give some idea of the intensity of the bombardment.

After the battle I was still in the O.P. and by the evening things had quietened down a bit. I looked out of the observing slit to find the ground literally covered with dead bodies. In the distance I could see a derelict tank, and after dark I decided to go down and have a look at it. One of my signallers volunteered to come with me and we cautiously approached the tank in case there were any snipers about. The door was open and I climbed in. Once inside I was surprised to see a British Tommy standing at the far end. He was a red-headed young fellow belonging to some Scottish regiment.

I said: "Hello, what are you doing here?"

I got no reply, so I walked down the length of the tank to where he was standing, wedged between some pieces of machinery. I then realised that he was stone dead. It was a pretty shattering experience.

While I was in this particular O.P. I had a request from divisional H.Q. to go out at night and search the dead, of which there were many hundreds. It was necessary to carry out this gruesome and macabre operation at night because of enemy snipers. The object of the exercise was to collect their identity discs and any personal effects.

I wasn't very keen on the idea, but it was an order and it had to be done. So the following night I went out with a couple of signallers and walked a few hundred yards from the Observing Post. The whole area was absolutely littered with dead, and it just gave me the "willies."

Anyway, we got to the first poor devil and took his identity disc, papers and valuables and put them in a little sandbag. We then went on to the next body and in this way managed to do about fifteen to twenty a night. We were constantly interruped by the enemy firing Very lights, which necessitated flinging ourselves on the ground to dodge possible sniping.

After about a week we'd collected quite a stack of sandbags full of these personal effects, so I rang up Divisional H.Q. and asked them to arrange to collect them as they were cluttering up the dug-out. The chap on the other end of the line then said that they would like me to get the home address of each casualty and write a letter to his relatives. I told him that I had no time to do this as I was supposed to be watching the Hun, and in any case I didn't think I was the right person for this very delicate job. So it was left like that and eventually they sent for the stuff.

One of my gun crew at this time was a young fellow called Ainsworth. One day we were being shelled heavily, and he decided to bolt. I shouted at him to stop and drew my revolver, threatening to shoot him, as this sort of thing could create a very dangerous situation, leading to panic. The morale of the men was pretty low at the time and incidents like this had to be dealt with promptly and severely. Ainsworth was in tears after the incident, and I took him on one side and asked him what the trouble was. He said that he was just petrified with fear and couldn't control himself. I told him that we all felt like that to a greater or lesser degree, but we just had to take a pull on ourselves. I then told him that in order to give him a change I was going to take him on as my batman. He seemed to like the idea.

A couple of days later I took him up to the O.P. with me, and the following morning he brought my tea. It was pitch black and had a filthy taste. I called Ainsworth and asked him where he got the water to make the tea.

He answered: "From the stream, Sir," Apparently the water that came up with the rations had run out.

I said: "Right, show me where you got it," as I couldn't remember any stream near the O.P.

He then confessed that he'd got it from a shell hole, very close to the O.P. So I asked him to show me which shell hole it was. It transpired that there were three dead Germans in the shell hole in an advanced state of decomposition. No wonder the tea tasted so foul! I tore strips off poor Ainsworth, who was most contrite, but I could see he was never going to be any good as a soldier.

The following day he and I went down to the wagon line and the C.O. decided to get Ainsworth evacuated as a shell shock case, and he was sent back to the U.K. His was just one of the many cases that one came across — chaps that simply couldn't take it. I think that poor Ainsworth's background had something to do with it, as he was an only son of a widowed mother.

The ceaseless assault on Passchendaele went on and, interminably, on, with very little progress being made. The number of times that I escaped death confirmed my theory that one's life is ordained. I remember one occasion particularly.

We were ordered to carry out an intense bombardment on a German position and I, as orderly officer, had to supervise this. I went across to alert the gun crews in their dug-out, and the sergeant-major who was to assist me was shaving. So I told him to get on with his shave and I would do the job myself. I got the gun crews into their positions and was just waiting for the predetermined time to open fire. Orders were being shouted down from the control post, and at that moment the sergeant-major joined me with the shaving soap lather still on his face. I asked him why he hadn't finished his shaving, and he replied: "It's my job, Sir, and I must do it."

The noise from the guns was so deafening that I couldn't hear the orders coming from the control post, so I said to the S.M.: "Carry on, and I'll go and see what it's all about."

I'd gone about thirty yards when I heard a loud explosion behind me. Looking back I saw the S.M. lying on the ground. I dashed back and as I reached him I could see that he was badly wounded. I picked him up and rested his head on my knee. As I spoke to him his head fell back, his jaw dropped open and I could see that he was dead.

If the S.M. hadn't been so conscientious I would have "copped it" and not him. The sad part was that the day before as he and I were going round the guns, he had told me with great glee that he was to be repatriated to England as he had been in France for three years, and how he was looking forward to joining his wife and three children. It seemed so unfair that it should have been him, a family man, and not me, a young bachelor with no responsibilities. Life, especially in war-time, can be very cruel.

On July 30, 1917, we received orders that a terrific attack was to be launched at dawn the next day. This was to be an all-out attempt finally to take the notorious Passchendaele Ridge.

Sitting in the dug-out the night before the attack one of my brother officers and I were chatting. He was a young Canadian called Cambridge, who had recently joined our battery.

I was detailed to go over the top with half-a-dozen signallers accompanying the infantry who were going to make the initial attack. Cambridge was to come along later with the support troops.

I realised that it was going to be a prettty tough assignment, but I had been detailed to do it, so that was that.

However, during our talk the previous evening young Cambridge said to me: "I think it's unfair that we Canadians shouldn't have a chance of going over with the front-line troops. You've already done more than your bit, having been in the war so long. Now it's up to us."

I told him that as I'd been detailed to do the job there was not much chance of changing it. However, we discussed it with the C.O. who agreed that we could settle it between us.

So Cambridge and I tossed for it. He won the toss and to my surprise he chose to go over with the front-line troops. I would therefore replace him and go over with the support troops. We went up the line at three the next morning. A most ghastly bombardment was in progress and there was general confusion.

Anyhow, this attack commenced and I gathered Cambridge and his signallers went forward. Neither he nor they were ever seen or heard of again. I imagine that they were simply blown to pieces. Once again I'd had a very narrow escape.

I went up with the support troops ana after some hours of bloody Hell we took and occupied Passchendaele Ridge at last.

We then realised why it had been so difficult to occupy. The Germans had converted the whole ridge into an almost impregnable fortress, so that our bombardments had had little or no effect on them. It was the most extraordinary place. Lit by electric light with galleries, beds and all mod cons — in fact a veritable underground village.

We had been told that once we got on the ridge the terrain beyond would be more or less flat, and that we'd have no difficulty in continuing the advance. However, once I got on the ridge I could see nothing but undulating country, with a few Germans who had escaped capture "legging it" back in the general direction of Berlin. Owing to the number of casualties we'd sustained, plus the difficult terrain, any thought of further advance was shelved for the time being.

My relief found his way to the ridge and I returned to the gun line, bloody lucky to be alive. We had suffered three hundred and fifty thousand casualties.

Passchendaele was to be my Swan Song as far as France was concerned.

In the gun line we were occupying a captured German dug-out which was, as far we we were concerned, facing the wrong way. It was well constructed with about fifteen steps leading to the surface. One morning I came up to "see a man about a dog." I'd gone a yard or so when I heard a shell coming, and from long experience I knew it was going to land pretty close. I flung myself on the ground and there was a terrific explosion. The next thing I knew was that I was lying on a stretcher in the dug-out with the doctor bending over me.

"You've been bloody lucky, young fella," said the doctor. He then told me that the force of the explosion had blown me down the steps and back into the dug-out, but that I hadn't been seriously wounded or injured. However, he said that I had been pretty badly shocked and suggested that I should have ten days leave in the U.K. — a suggestion with which I heartily concurred.

6

Marriage and desertion

The next day, in a state of shock and still feeling completely dazed, I was evacuated to England. I remember very little of the journey, but on arrival in London I was asked where I would like to go. As I had a girlfriend in Belfast I asked to be sent there. By the time I got to Ireland I had developed the most violent stomach pain, which turned out to be a burst appendix. So instead of going to stay with my fiancée's parents, I was put into a private nursing home and immediately had an emergency operation.

In the next bed to me was a Captain McGill of the Irish Fusiliers. He had been caught in machine-gun fire and had sixteen bullet wounds. On this particular morning McGill was in great pain, and asked me if I could get a nurse. The old tyrant of a matron wouldn't allow us to have bells, and the only way I could communicate was by banging a shoe on the floor. This I did and caused a considerable noise. Nothing happened for a few minutes and then there was an unusual sound. To our amazement the matron sort of "tobogganed" into the room on her bottom! She had apparently slipped on the landing at the top of the stairs. This undignified entrance did nothing to improve her temper. She stood up, adjusted her uniform, and in a very haughty voice demanded: "Who made that noise?"

I explained that I had done it on Captain McGill's behalf, because he was desperately in need of attention.

Matron told me that as I obviously didn't know how to behave myself I would be sent to a military hospital. She then turned her wrath on poor McGill. He took the wind out of her sails by saying that from then on he would have his own doctor and his own nurse. I heard after the war that poor McGill had died as a result of an operation for a duodenal ulcer.

The matron wasn't to get rid of me as easily as she had hoped. Complications developed and it was some weeks before I could be moved to the military hospital. In the meantime, our relationship improved, and I flatter myself that she was quite sorry when I was moved.

The burst appendix was really a blessing in disguise, as I realised after a couple of weeks in hospital what a shocking state I was in, both mentally and physically. Every time a tram went past in the street below I would try to get out of the window. The noise of the tram coming up the street seemed in my confused state of mind to be very like a shell arriving. Added to this, owing to my low state of health, my appendix wound took six weeks to heal.

Whether it was due to shell shock or not I don't know, but my beautiful Irish fiancée and I decided to get married while I was still in hospital. I was only twenty-one, but life was so uncertain in those days, and the threat of my being sent back to France was always hanging over us.

The medical authorities expressed some concern over the proposed wedding and only allowed the ceremony to take place on condition that I came straight back to the nursing home afterwards!

So Florence May McConnell and I were married in a little church in Fort William, followed by a small luncheon party at the local hotel. Subsequently, the bridegroom was packed into a taxi and sent back to the nursing home to bed — alone!

Despite its inauspicious beginning our marriage lasted for fifty-seven happy years.

Three weeks later I was well enough to be moved to the military hospital at Hollywood, on the coast, north of Belfast. I was still an "in" patient, but the authorities were very considerate and I was allowed a good deal of freedom.

In due course I was transferred to what was known as a convalescent camp, at Ripon in Yorkshire. We felt rather like animals being fattened up ready to be sent back to the slaughterhouse in France. As a married officer I was allowed to live in an hotel nearby. Part of the treatment was rowing up the river Ure, and other relaxing forms of exercise.

After six weeks at Ripon, and having medical examinations every week, I was declared category C3, and as such unfit to return to duty. To our joy the War Office decided to send me back to Belfast for temporary employment under the Ministry of Labour. I had an office in the main street of Belfast, and my job was to re-settle permanently unfit men from the army into civilian jobs. This suited us admirably, as we were able to stay with my wife's sister who lived nearby. This saved us having to pay for accommodation, which was a big factor, as my pay at the time was ten shillings per day.

At that time the army wouldn't recognise an officer under the age of thirty as being married. If you married under that age you simply had to manage on a single officer's pay. As far as the army was concerned you were living in sin! I hadn't realised that when I decided to get married. Not that it would have made any difference, but it would have made the next few years a lot more comfortable.

By the end of October 1918 it was obvious that the war was coming to an end, and I received orders to join a field regiment in the Aldershot Command. I made arrangements to leave Belfast on November 11 and carried on despite the fact that Armistice Day wasn't the ideal time to travel. Everywhere people were going crazy with joy, dancing in the streets, shouting, singing and kissing every chap in uniform. Two girls from Gallaghar's tobacco factory even tried to remove my pants! I got to London later that day and everything was even more chaotic. I was wearing my 1914 medal ribbon and my blue hospital armband and was positively mobbed by the girls wherever I went. Anyone would think I'd won the war single-handed!

Anyway, it was all very flattering and gratifying. I spent a couple of nights with my mother, who was very upset about my marriage. My youth, plus the fact that I hadn't consulted her before "committing the offence" seemed to be the trouble. I could see that my wife was going to have a hostile reception when the inevitable meeting took place. However, I staved it off for the time being by taking my wife straight down to Deepcut when she eventually came over from Ireland.

I had been in Deepcut for about a month when the adjutant said he wanted me to take a draft consisting of about one hundred and fifty N.C.O s and men over to France.

We proceeded to Southampton where we boarded a huge American liner which had been converted into a troopship. I'd never seen such an enormous ship. It was carrying some thousands of black and white "doughboys."

My men were carrying only the unexpired portion of their day's ration, as we expected to be in Le Havre in a matter of hours. I reported to the American general commanding the ship and we sailed for France. In mid-channel we hove-to on account of thick fog, and there we stayed for two days! I was given grub in the American officer's mess, but on the first morning when I went down to inspect my men, the N.C.O. in charge of the draft told me that they had run out of rations. So at breakfast that morning I explained our predicament to the American general. He agreed to supply us with grub, but said that on arrival in Le Havre he would expect some form of payment.

I told him that I had no money, but I would give him a letter to the authorities. However, whether he'd ever get paid was another matter!

The night before we arrived in Le Havre the Yanks announced that they were going to put on a concert, and the general asked me if any of my men could do a turn. They would particularly like a Harry Lauder act. I said that I didn't really know, but I'd try and find out. So I went down into the bowels of the ship and got hold of my senior N.C.O. in charge of the draft, and asked him if he could help. He replied that we had a chap who could impersonate Harry Lauder perfectly. So I said, "Let's have a look at him." He produced this fellow and I must say he was the spittin' image of

Harry Lauder. He was a wee Scot by the name of McPherson, complete with kilt and crooked stick. He was only too happy to do his stuff at the concert.

In due course he came on the stage to do his turn. He was absolutely terrific, and I think he would have fooled even Harry Lauder himself. The Americans went beserk and wouldn't let him off the stage, and, mainly due to McPherson, the concert was a great success.

Next morning at breakfast the American general said to me: "That was a very, very good show your men put on last night. In fact, I'm so pleased that we will waive any question of payment for rations."

I thanked him very much and we duly landed at Le Havre, and proceeded with my draft to a place called Harfleur, where there was a big reinforcement camp. I handed over the draft and reported to the adjutant chap.

"Any orders?" I said, expecting to be told to return to the U.K. as I was still category C3.

Instead the adjutant replied: "Hang around for a few days and we'll find something for you to do."

I wasn't very happy about this. However, I went along to the officers' mess and got talking to a young infantry officer who was in the same boat as myself.

He said: "I can't see much point in us hanging about here, I'm going to try and get back to England. We'll just be loafing about doing nothing. The war's just about finished. Let's see what we can do."

So we went down to the docks and there was a ship — a sort of paddle-steamer — tied up at the quayside. My friend and conspirator said he thought this vessel would suit us. We didn't dare board it in the normal way, so we swung onto the ship by means of one of the hawsers. As we dropped onto the deck of the ship I heard a shout, apparently from one of the military police who had spotted us. We bolted down below, he into one cabin and I into another. I got into a bunk and covered myself with blankets. Presently I heard voices, and realised that it was the M.P s searching the ship and trying to find out who we were. They came into my cabin, where I was pretending to be asleep.

"No, that's not the bloke we're looking for," they said, much to my relief, and pushed off.

I heard them going into the other fellow's cabin, and after a bit of a scuffle, took him away.

In due course the military police came back to my cabin again, but they were still convinced that I wasn't the chap they were looking for and, presently to my intense relief, I heard the ship's engines starting up, and off we went to Blighty. What happened to my partner in crime I never discovered.

We arrived in England and I went up to London to my mother's place, where my wife was staying. Diplomatic relations between the two women were extremely strained. My wife was very worried when she heard what had happened, as it was tantamount to desertion. However, my conscience was quite clear as I felt that I'd more than done my bit, and that loafing about in Harfleur was just a waste of time, although legally I suppose I had committed an offence. I must admit that I was more than worried about how the situation would develop when I got back to Deepcut, and my wife expected me to be led away under police escort at any minute.

However, we set off for Deepcut where I had managed to find accommodation with the local carpenter. I reported to the adjutant with my heart in the general direction of my mouth, half expecting to see a firing squad standing by!

"Well Hodgson, everything all right?" asked the adjutant.

"Yes, everything fine, and we had a luxury trip in an American liner," I replied.

"Good, well, there's plenty of work for you here, as you're to take over the demobbing section."

The adjutant made no further reference to my trip to France, and I got down to the job of demobbing hundreds of chaps, who couldn't get out of the army quickly enough.

No sooner had we settled down at Deepcut and moved into quite a nice house than I received orders to report to Woolwich. While travelling by train to Woolwich I happened to buy the Daily Telegraph. In the paper there was a War Office announcement to the effect that all regular officers under the age of thirty who had married during the war would now be recognised officially as such and would be paid accordingly. This was the best bit of news we'd had since our marriage, and meant that my wife would no longer need to be a camp follower! From now on we would be able to live in some degree of comfort, and in the event of my being killed my wife would be eligible for a pension. In other words, in the eyes of the army, our marriage was now legal and our children, if any, would be legitimate!

On arrival at the depot I was told that I was to join a division which was being formed to go to Archangel in Russia to support the White Russians against the Bolsheviks.

For my wife's sake I wasn't very enthusiastic about this venture, as it would mean leaving her with my mother again for an indefinite period. The preparations were to take about three months, and we started to mobilise and train. After about a month of training the C.O. came to me one day and said: "Hodgson, I believe you're very keen on riding?"

I replied that that was so. In fact, I added, I was more than keen. He told me that he had to send an officer to Weedon on a two-year course to be trained as a riding instructor, and asked if I would like to go. "At least you won't have to go to Russia," he said. Of course I jumped at the chance, and as soon as possible set out for Weedon in Northants to make arrangements about accommodation and so on.

I managed to find two rooms with the use of the kitchen, in the local manor house, which was owned by a very pleasant widow. There was stabling for my horses and we had the use of the garden. So we settled in and spent two happy years at Weedon.

When my wife saw the enormous kitchen with its formidable-looking coal range, she expressed some alarm, but promised to do her best. She was of the generation that had been brought up with a culinary knowledge that hardly included boiling an egg. The first few weeks were pretty grim food-wise, but luckily I was able to get my lunch in the mess, so managed to escape some of the culinary disasters.

We were obliged to take one horse with us to Weedon. My

charger at Woolwich was a South American horse by the name of Mrs. Woo. Although she was excellent as a charger and hunter, she unfortunately got carnivorous tendencies when it came to her grooms.

For example, I was on parade one day when I got a message asking me to go to the stable as there had been an accident. I found my groom Spendlove writhing in agony, with blood pouring from his head. Mrs. Woo had bitten his ear off. She used to go beserk at feeding time and had to be fed from the adjacent stall. We rushed Spendlove off to the hospital and then searched the bedding for his ear so that the doctor could stitch it on again. This search was without success, so we presumed that Mrs. Woo had swallowed the ear.

I wanted to take Mrs. Woo to Weedon, but had to find a new groom with sufficient courage to cope with her vicious behaviour. I found a chap called Forder, who agreed to take on Mrs. Woo and he took her up to Weedon by rail. I felt that if the riding school couldn't cure her temperament nothing could, as we talked, breathed and lived horses twelve hours a day. It was felt that Mrs. Woo's behaviour was entirely due to the way she had been handled in the past. One aspect of her treatment was to turn her loose, but knee-haltered, in the paddock, and to feed and groom her while she was there. This seemed to work admirably and we thought we'd solved the problem. However, it was not to be.

One morning I was sitting on the lawn when Forder appeared in great distress and told me that Mrs. Woo had bitten him. He had a very nasty wound on his side. However, Forder stuck it out in spite of his difficult assignment, which pleased me very much as Mrs. Woo really was a wonderful hunter, and once out of the stable was no trouble at all.

7

Hunting, hacking and horses

On arrival at Weedon we were given two horses. One was fully trained and the other had just been "backed" (ridden for the first time). All the horses at Weedon were "in the book", which meant that they were thoroughbreds. I expect they gave Mrs Woo a bit of an inferiority complex!

The idea was that you would learn all your riding on the trained horse, and, as you progressed, the knowledge that you had acquired would be used to train the other horse. This meant that by the end of the year, when the hunting season started, I would have three perfectly trained horses to hunt. As students at the riding school we had the privilege of hunting, at a very reduced rate, with all the famous local packs, like Pytchley, Grafton, Quorn and North Warwick. We only paid what was known as a "Cap" of one guinea per hunt. To distinguish "odds and sods" like us from the members of the hunt "elite" we were not permitted to wear the traditional pink coats. Our hunting kit consisted of top hat, white cravat, white waistcoat, black hunting coat, brown riding breeches, black hunting boots with spurs and the traditional hunting crop. Although "I sez it meself," we looked quite smart.

While I had done a fair amount of riding before going to Weedon in order to get myself toughened up, being in the saddle for six hours a day was a different story. Before long my "post extremis" became so sore that I visualised feeding off the mantelpiece for the rest of my life! One morning in the stable I spoke to my groom about my seating problem.

I said: "My bottom is so bloody sore, I can't sit down. Can you suggest anything?"

"Yes Sir," he said. "What you should do is to blanco your bottom every day and you'll find it'll heal up and get really hard."

So the groom and I retired to a secluded part of the stable and made the first application, a somewhat undignified procedure for a gunner officer! Another suggestion that he made was to wear a pair of ladies silk stockings with the feet cut off in order to prevent soreness of the knees. Happily, after a week of my groom's rather unconventional treatment, I was able to stay in the saddle *ad infinitum* with no discomfort.

One of the methods used at the school for toughening us up was to make us ride the wooden horse. This "animal" was operated by remote control, so that the rider never knew what it was going to do next. It could be made to buck, rear, trot, canter and gallop at the touch of a button, and it was made of some hard material. If one was thrown onto its neck it was quite painful, but it did improve one's balance and grip. Another part of the toughening-up process was the gymnasium where we did all the usual exercises such as vaulting, rope climbing and fencing — sabre v. sabre. The latter made us very agile and quick on our feet.

One of our outdoor exercises was learning to vault into the saddle while the horse was cantering along, a stunt that I'd always associated with circuses.

After three months of intensive exercise my weight had dropped to nine stone of solid muscle and I was as fit as a flea. We also had our own steeple-chase course, which we usually rode every day.

To my mind, the only really terrifying part of the course was what was known as "riding the Big Lane". This consisted of about eight jumps in the form of an enclosed lane. The jumps were above average in height and fixed. The course had to be ridden without reins or stirrups so that everything was left to the horse. Owing to the inherent danger of the Big Lane we were told that it was "voluntary," but of course it was more than your life at

Weedon was worth NOT to volunteer! It was while riding this horrific course that I missed death once again, literally by inches this time.

I was riding my favourite horse Wentworth, who was normally an exceptional jumper, and on coming to "The Wall" he misjudged his take-off, hit the top and turned a complete somersault, throwing me over the wall in the process. I landed flat on my back and was winded. As I lay there I could hear the next horse thundering down the lane, and realised that I was in considerable danger. I decided to lie still, and believe it or not, as the horse landed he took my hat off with his left fore. To support my story, I was able to show the imprint of the horse's hoof on my felt hat, which I kept as a souvenir for many years.

In order to improve our riding techniques we were fined one shilling every time we were thrown. As our average pay was only ten shillings per day this was quite a deterrent! I managed to get away with only paying twelve shillings for the whole course.

A three-month course in veterinary work was another very important part of our training. We were taught all about the various ailments to which horses were prone, and how to cure them. Here again we had a model of a horse which could be taken to pieces, showing various parts of its anatomy in detail. The knowledge that I acquired then stood me in very good stead, particularly when I was in India, and had a number of horses of my own. I was able to cope in the absence of a vet when I was stationed in some of the smaller cantonments.

Another interesting part of the course was show-jumping. Once we'd completed this we were allowed to compete in local shows, and test our ability against the Northamptonshire riders.

When autumn came, the prospect of fox hunting became the talk of the day. This was an exciting and completely new world to me, and, but for the army, would have been quite out of my reach financially. I realised how lucky I was to be given this marvellous opportunity.

Prior to the actual hunting came "Cubbing" and "Badger Digging." This involved filling in the fox-holes and badger burrows, to prevent the fox "going to ground" during the hunt. Regrettably this also meant killing some badgers and fox cubs. A more pleasant side of the badger digging exercise was that we were nearly always invited to a marvellous lunch at some baronial hall.

Once the hunting season got under way, I was sometimes able to hunt three times a week, using my three horses — Wendy, Wentworth and Mrs. Woo — in turn.

Depending on the distance away from Weedon that the "meet" took place, we could choose the pack with which we wanted to hunt. As we had to hack to the meet, it had to be reasonably near.

One occasion in particular that I remember was when I took Mrs. Woo to hunt with the Pytchley. The meet was some fifteen miles away. The M.F.H. blew his horn and off we went on an unusually long point of fifteen miles. At one stage this seemed to be too much for Mrs. Woo and she started fighting for her head, so I gave her full rein and she continued to gallop with her head well down. This nearly proved fatal, as we suddenly came onto a stream with Mrs. Woo completely out of balance.

To "collect" her would have been disastrous, so I shut my eyes and left it to her. Old Ma Woo made a gallant effort to clear the stream, but unfortunately crashed into the high bank on the other side, and went base over apex, throwing me in the process. Landing on my back, I managed to hang on to the reins as we'd been taught at Weedon. But with the other horses galloping past, Mrs. Woo took fright, jerked the reins out of my hands and careered off to join the hunt. I'd pretty well given up both the hunt and horse when a hunt servant appeared and asked if he could help.

"Yes," I said gratefully, "that's my horse disappearing over the hill. Do you think you can catch her?"

In a short time he reappeared leading Mrs. Woo. Having removed a large portion of the ploughed field which I'd collected in the fall, I remounted and the hunt servant and I galloped off to catch up with the hunt.

I arrived literally "at the kill," where they were presenting the youngest female member of the hunt with the fox's "brush," or tail. After this ceremony was over I decided that, as I only had one horse, I'd better think about getting back to Weedon. I pulled out, and after a short rest set off on the eighteen mile journey home. Luckily I had some company in the form of an attractive young woman member of the hunt who lived in the next village. We arrived at dusk and Mrs. Woo was still going strong, although beginning to stumble a bit from exhaustion after her forty-eight-mile trip. However, she was not too tired to have a go at her groom when we fed her in her stall as usual. The Weedon course certainly produced fitness both in men and horses.

Of course, this was the Bertie Wooster era of cucumber sand-wiches and tea on the lawn, with a game of croquet with the vicar thrown in! I became quite friendly with the local croquet cham-pion who introduced me to the game, and on one occasion I even managed to beat him, much to his disgust! Anyway, it was a relaxing change from hacking, hunting and horses.

Mixed hockey was another form of relaxation and one that I found highly dangerous! We didn't have a proper hockey field and used to play in a paddock belonging to one of the local farmers. The only snag was that the field was also used for grazing his cows! One day, during a hard-fought game, I found the ball resting on a large lump of cow dung. I understood that the ball had to be played from where it rested, so I played it, with dis-astrous results to my opponent and myself!

There was a horse at Weedon that was untrainable and un-rideable. I nicknamed it "the rubber horse." It threw everyone who mounted it, and as a punishment for being "a bad boy" the in-structor would detail the offender to ride it. One day a chap called Captain Ian Campbell, who subsequently got the V.C. in the North Africa campaign, said that he would teach this horse a lesson. The horse was led out and young Campbell got aboard. He was a very tall chap in the Horse Artillery, and his feet were not very far from the ground when he sat on the horse. He managed to stay aboard much longer than most of us, but eventually even he was thrown.

A tragic note about Ian Campbell and his V.C.: On the way to the investiture — also in North Africa — he was involved in a car accident and killed. He was a brigadier at the time.

After the Weedon course I was posted to a battery at Norwich in Norfolk, a delightful cathedral city. It was a two-battery station, the other two being in Ipswich. I was immediately landed with the job of training officers and men in equitation. We had a good indoor riding school, as it had originally been a cavalry barracks.

After I had been in Norwich a short time we received a batch of "remounts." These were horses that had been trained but had never been in a unit. Believe it or not, who should be among them but the "rubber horse" from Weedon that nobody could ride. Of course, I spotted it immediately, and told the chaps in the mess about the "unrideable horse." They told me I was talking rubbish and said: "Bring him round and let's have a look at this bronco."

So I had him saddled and one of the young chaps got aboard. Sure enough, within a couple of minutes he was back on terra firma, the laughing stock of the mess. As the horse was unsuitable for gun team work, being too light, we regrettably had to have him put down.

One day we were informed that the Brigadier Royal Artillery was coming on his annual inspection. Pandemonium reigned for days as we prepared for this. Rehearsals became the order of the day, and hours were spent spitting and polishing. The great day arrived and the whole regiment was on parade, boots shining and buttons gleaming. As the B.R.A. rode on to the parade ground the general salute was sounded by a mounted trumpeter.

However, the salute came to an abrupt halt as the trumpeter's horse suddenly bolted across the parade ground at full tilt and disappeared in a cloud of dust. It was quite some time before the quaking trumpeter and his horse could be recovered and brought before the irate B.R.A.

"Have you got a Weedon-trained officer here?" barked the B.R.A. to my C.O., who rejoiced in the name of Major Twisleton-Wykham-Fiennes.

"Yes Sir," the Major replied, "Hodgson!"

Whereupon, feeling rather like Exhibit A, I was produced, and told to retrain the trumpeter's horse in time for the next inspection. After persevering for some time it was decided that he was untrainable (the horse, not the B.R.A.) and the trumpeter was given a more suitable mount.

Part of our regimental equipment at Norwich was a coach and four, the sort of conveyance that you normally associate with Christmas cards. We used this form of transport to get ourselves to the local horse shows and other sporting events. In those days hardly anyone in the army could afford a car, and there were very few on the roads.

While at Norwich I organised and trained a polo team, something of a rarity in England at that time. We were indebted to an aircraft manufacturing company called Boulton and Paul who allowed us to use their airfield as a polo ground. Our standard wasn't exactly international, but it was good fun and practice for my future life in India. They also allowed us to build a small steeple-chase course round the edge of the aerodrome, on Mousehold Heath.

I became very friendly with a young officer called Pelham-Burn, who had ambitions to ride in the Grand Military. This was the military equivalent of the Grand National, and was the goal of most young army riders. To this end Pelham-Burn bought a horse on the open market in Norwich, and asked me to vet it. I was not very impressed, but agreed to ride with him over the steeple-chase course.

After a few days' practice in the closed menage we went up to the steeple-chase course on Mousehold Heath. As he took the first two fences it was pretty obvious that the horse had no idea of how to jump. However, as Pelham-Burn was determined to ride this animal we persevered with the training, to very little effect. As the day of the race drew near I tried my best to persuade P-B to withdraw his entry as I felt he was running too big a risk. But he was adamant. The day before he left for Sandown it was obvious that he had misgivings as he handed all his private papers over to me, with instructions on how to dispose of them should the worst happen.

On the day of the steeple-chase I was very uneasy, and with good reason. In those days there was no radio commentary, but we heard later in the day that poor P-B had fallen at the second fence and was seriously injured. He was severely concussed and remained unconscious for six months. He did recover to some extent, but had to be invalided out of the service. The whole thing seemed so unnecessary and I was very sad that such a promising young officer should have had his career ended in this way.

Norwich seemed to abound in "horsey" characters. One of these was a chap called Selby-Lowndes, who came from a well-known hunting family in South England. He lived and breathed horses and was a bit of a "coper" on the side.

Selby-Lowndes went to the Horse Fair in Norwich one day and came back with a most magnificent-looking animal that he had bought for only fifty pounds. We all gathered round to admire this beautiful horse with its flowing mane and tail. I felt that there must be a snag somewhere for him to have got such a bargain, but could find nothing wrong.

Selby sold the horse on the spot to another officer for seventy-five pounds, and so made himself a quick profit. However, there was a snag — a big one. When we took him out of his stable the next morning he was walking like a cat on hot bricks. I quickly diagnosed lamynitis, a disease of the hoof which was incurable. The horse had obviously been doped the day before to fool the buyer. The new owner was naturally furious as he felt he'd been "sold a pup," but I'm sure Selby had sold it in good faith. After a good deal of discussion it was agreed to cancel the sale and the horse was destroyed.

Norwich was a delightful station with many amenities, both cultural and sporting. We did a good deal of duck shooting on the Norfolk Broads and sailing on all of the many inland waterways. On one occasion I had the great pleasure of hearing Ernest Lough sing his famous "Oh! for the wings of a dove" in Norwich Cathedral.

All good things must eventually come to an end, and late in 1921 the regiment received orders to proceed to Dublin as mounted infantry in order to help quell the unrest in Ireland.

8

The bastard from Ballakinler

The notorious "Black and Tans" were much in evidence at this time and formed part of the force against the Sinn Feiners. The "Black and Tans" were so called because of the colour of their uniforms. It was a special force composed mainly of officers and men who had been demobilised after World War I and had difficulty finding employment. They proved invaluable for the job as they were as ruthless as the Sinn Feiners themselves.

The words "Sinn Fein" mean "we alone" in Gaelic, and was the name given by the Irish to their rebel army. They were backed by De Valera and Michael Collins.

Here again my luck was in. We had too many officers for the job in hand and in consequence I was given an appointment on the staff at H.Q. in Belfast, Northern Ireland. This was most welcome as my pay was doubled and we could live with my wife's sister in Belfast. However, it was too good to be true, as once in Belfast I was ordered to go to a place called Ballakinler, near the Irish town of Newcastle, "where the Mountains of Mourne sweep down to the sea." Ballakinler was a normal two-battalion peace station, but it had been developed into a huge P.O.W. camp, holding some three to four thousand Sinn Feiners. The camp was divided into four sections, each holding some eight hundred and fifty "Shinners," as we called them. My job was to administer one of these sections. The inmates were treated as prisoners of war under the Geneva Convention, and had their own officers and N.C.O.s.

I relieved a Captain Dundass of the Black Watch, who couldn't make a go of it. The Shinners couldn't stand the Scots and for that reason wouldn't co-operate with Dundass, and made his task impossible.

My first job on arrival at Ballakinler was to make the acquaintance of the Sinn Fein commandant of my section of the camp. On entering the camp I was escorted by two armed sentries with fixed bayonets. Once in the commandant's office he stood up and saluted, although he wore the uniform of a brigadier in the Sinn Fein Army and I was a mere lieutenant. His main concern seemed to be my nationality — was I English? I was able to reassure him on that point, and he seemed to think that, for this reason, we would get on better than was the case with my Scottish predecessor.

There were no married quarters at the camp, but despite this my wife insisted on coming with me to Ballakinler. I was a bit apprehensive about it, but once having made up her mind there was no stopping her. She wasn't Irish for nothing!

We eventually found accommodation for her at a little place called Dundrum. From the cottage where she was to live you could see Ballakinler camp, about a mile across the bay. I was very uneasy about my wife living there. I felt that should the Shinners find out that she was there they might abduct her or worse, particularly as she was an Irish woman consorting with the "enemy."

For my wife's safety and protection I devised a scheme. She was to keep a lamp burning in her cottage window, day and night. This light could be seen from our guard-room, and part of the sentry's duty was always to keep it in view, and to raise the alarm if it ever went out. Should the light go out I would take half-a-dozen troops, cross the bay by ferry and investigate.

Thank goodness the occasion never arose, but I admired my wife's courage in living under these conditions.

Escape from Ballakinler was the first priority of every Shinner in the camp. The security arrangements were top class, with two

58

belts of barbed wire and sentries in towers overlooking the camp. We thought that escape was impossible, but they proved us wrong on two occasions while I was there.

On the first occasion I was really "caught for a sucker." As normal routine I went into the camp every evening with my two armed sentries to call the roll. Each hut contained about twenty-five men, and we visited each in turn, the whole operation taking a couple of hours. When we got to one of the huts there was no reply from two of the men.

"Sure and Be Jebus he's sick now," said the hut leader, taking me along to view the body.

Sure enough there was a man in bed, asleep. I pulled the blanket back to make sure, and left it at that.

The same thing happened with the next man, and I went on to the next hut.

I suppose I should have been suspicious because the hut leader was so unusually co-operative. At the conclusion of the roll call I went back to the mess and then to bed.

About 2 a.m. the following morning I was woken up by an orderly from my commandant saying: "The Commandant's compliments Sir, will you come at once?" I threw on some clothes and went with him to the C.O.'s quarters.

Without any preliminaries the C.O. said: "Did you call the roll last night?"

"Yes Sir," I replied.

"Everything correct?"

"Yes Sir, except that there were two men sick in bed."

"And did you identify them?"

"Yes Sir, as best I could."

In a very sarcastic voice the C.O. then said: "For your information two of your men have been captured between Newry and Drogheda. I suggest that you go back and call the roll again."

Feeling a "proper Charlie" I went back into the camp, and straight to the hut where the sick men had been. Sure enough, on going to their beds, and pulling the blankets right back, I found that the two "sick men" were in fact extremely well-made dummies. Looking up at the hut leader who had a smirk on his face reminiscent of "the cat who swallowed the canary," I just walked out of the hut with a very red face. By this time all the other inmates of the hut were awake and smirking and jeering as I walked out.

Crawling back to the C.O.'s quarters went a very contrite and humiliated lieutenant.

I could only say in defence that the dummies were so good that they could have fooled anyone.

"Well, you're bloody lucky," said the C.O. "You'd have been for the high jump if they'd got away. You can thank your lucky stars and Captain Dundass that they didn't."

What had happened was this: Captain Dundass was out on patrol on the Drogheda road and had stopped a vehicle for a routine check. There were about twelve Irishmen in it. He lined them up on the road to check their identity. He was suspicious of two and had them arrested. These two turned out to be my "sick men" from Ballakinler. They were brought back to the camp, court martialed and given thirty days solitary. The question was how they got out of the camp? Eventually the mystery was solved.

In each section there was a clinic manned by R.A.M.C. orderlies. Two of these men had been bribed by the Shinners to hand over their uniforms. Wearing these uniforms, the two escapees marched boldly up to the main gate and asked to be let out. The sentry at the gate failed to carry out his job of identifying the two men. He was subsequently found to be involved in the plot, and the whole lot were punished accordingly.

A more ambitious escape plot was attempted later on in my camp. I was told by the intelligence people that an attempt was being made to escape by tunnelling, but they couldn't find out from which hut the tunnel started. They asked me to do a routine check. I was pretty certain I knew from which hut the tunnelling was being carried out so I went in one morning with some troops and cleared the hut of all bedding and everything else on the floor. Then I carried out a "Sherlock Holmes" inspection and went over every inch of the place but found Sweet Fanny Adams. The bedding and other things were left outside and I told the hut leader that he could now put it back. Believe it or not, that night when I went in to call the roll the bedding was still on the ground outside, and the Shinners were sitting on their bottoms on the floor. The temperature was well below freezing.

As I left the hut I said to the hut leader: "Why don't you put your stuff back in the hut?"

He replied, "You put it out, you can put it back."

"That will be the day," I said.

Those stubborn and fanatical Irishmen left their bedding outside for a week, by which time half of them had got pneumonia. At this stage the C.O. got cold feet and ordered me to have the bedding put back in the hut.

We were still concerned about the tunnelling and getting nowhere with our investigations. We couldn't understand how they were disposing of the sand that they were digging out of the tunnel. Sewage carts were searched, but to no purpose. Then fate took a hand. One morning there was a commotion outside my office. A lorry had got stuck as the road subsided under one of its rear wheels. The intelligence people realised that this was something to do with the tunnel but we pretended to know nothing about it. However, we realised that this would probably speed up the escape attempt, so steps were taken to patrol right round the camp, day and night.

At dusk one evening we noticed half-a-dozen cars parked in a small wood about a mile from the camp, so we were pretty certain that this was going to be the night. A company of infantry was deployed under cover in the vicinity, and sure enough at about 2 a.m. up popped a lone figure, followed by several others. The infantry closed in and after a bit of a scuffle they caught all six escapees. The cars beat it as soon as they saw that the game was up.

When we investigated the tunnel we found that the sides had been rivetted with wooden planks. Where had they got the planks? It was found that these were actually bed boards. Each man in the camp had three boards as part of his bedding, and each gave one for use in the tunnel. They had disposed of the sand by filling their pockets and sprinkling it when they were exercising. The tunnel was in fact under the hut that I suspected, but instead of making the conventional hole in the floor, they had cut through the floor boards right along three sides of the hut, and hinged it so that it was movable. I would like to add that building this tunnel was no mean feat of engineering. As Ballakinler Camp was practically on the seashore, the earth was in fact beach sand and extremely difficult to contain when tunnelling.

I couldn't help feeling rather sorry that all their hard work and ingenuity should have been in vain.

The four sections of the camp at Ballakinler were separated from each other by belts of barbed wire and "death walks." The latter were paths or alleyways between the belts of wire. Anyone using them would come under automatic fire from a machine gun, or from a sentry in one of the towers.

The Shinners were communicating with each other through the barbed wire, and instructions were issued that this must be stopped. They were told that if it continued they would run the risk of being shot.

One afternoon I received a message to go to my camp immediately as there had been an accident. I rushed over to the camp to find the place in absolute turmoil. Lying on the ground were two men who appeared to be dead. Kneeling round the two bodies were hundreds of their comrades, wailing, chanting, praying and reading their rosaries.

Many of them were dipping pieces of material into the victims' blood. I gathered that these two unfortunate chaps were now martyrs. At this stage I couldn't get any information out of the Shinners as they were in such a highly emotional state. In fact, I thought that at any moment they might turn on me, in spite of the fact that I had doubled my armed escort. Retreat seemed to be the wisest course.

It was only later that we learned what had happened. One of the sentries in his tower overlooking the camp had warned the prisoners to keep back from the barbed wire. Despite orders, they were still making contact with each other. While shouting his orders the sentry put his rifle on the sill of the tower and in so doing a shot was fired. He had no intention whatsoever of shooting anyone.

62

Of course there was a fearful row over the whole incident. The sentry was placed under arrest, and a court martial was to be arranged, consisting of seven British officers and six Irishmen, not necessarily Sin Feiners. In fact the court martial was held, but the sentry was not present, as we felt that his life would be in danger once he was identified by the Shinners.

The whole incident was made more serious by virtue of the fact that the first man killed was the Mayor of Cork, a chap called Tad Barry. By a most incredible chance the bullet passed through Barry and killed the man behind him.

The verdict of the court martial was "accidental death" and the young British Tommy was acquitted and transferred to England.

We were always up against the stubborn belligerency of the Shinners. One night I went in to call the roll. The procedure was that the two armed sentries walked into the hut and ordered arms, banging the butts of their rifles on the floor. This was the accepted signal for the Shinners to get to their feet.

On this occasion I walked into the hut and found all the inmates still sitting on their backsides and making no effort to stand up. I realised that trouble was brewing and turned to the hut leader who was standing at the door smoking a cigarette (which was contrary to the rules) and looking most aggressive. He was a huge raw-boned Irishman over six feet tall, and held the rank of corporal.

I asked him what the trouble was and he deliberately failed to answer. So I said: "If you don't obey the rules you must accept the consequences."

I left the camp and reported to the commandant.

He said: "We must take immediate action to prevent this trouble spreading; I'll send over a company of infantry."

In due course a company of the 60th Rifles in light battle order with fixed bayonets appeared outside the hut where I was waiting. They were under the command of a Captain Trowbridge, son of Admiral Trowbridge, R.N. I could see that the troops were smacking their lips in anticipation of a fight. Having put Trowbridge in the picture we went into the hut.

The hut leader was still standing at the entrance smoking, and the rest of the inmates were still in their recumbent posture. Trowbridge made some remark to the hut leader, who then took the cigarette out of his mouth and blew the smoke into Trowbridge's face. This was too much for him, and being an ex-rugger Blue, he sailed into the hut leader and knocked him flat on his back.

Troops were moved into the hut and told to take up their positions behind each Shinner. I then spoke to them and said: "I'm going to call the roll again, and any man who fails to answer in the correct manner will be 'assisted' by the British Tommies."

I called the first name in Gaelic, as we were expected to do. Nothing happened, so I repeated it, still with no effect, so Seamus O'Leary had to be "assisted" to his feet, which I'm sure he found very painful.

After about half-a-dozen similar efforts, all hell broke loose and it became a free-for-all. Order was eventually restored and the roll-call carried out.

There were approximately thirty huts and the same procedure had to be followed at each hut, so roll-call on this occasion took most of the night.

One of the huts was occupied by old men who had been rebelling against British rule for many years. I was uneasy about giving them the same treatment as the others, so I went into the hut alone and spoke to the leader, a very elderly man, and said. "I don't want to treat you old men as we have the others. Be sensible and obey the rules of the camp."

The old chap said: "Give me five minutes and I'll let you know. I want to discuss it with my friends."

I went out of the hut and waited. In less than the stipulated time he appeared at the door and said there would be no trouble. The roll-call went off peacefully. After this incident relations between us and the Shinners were somewhat strained for some time as many of them had to get medical treatment for the bayonet wounds received from the 60th Rifles. I reckon they deserved them for their mulish stubbornness.

Everything that went in and out of the camp was strictly censored. Files and small saws were often found in cakes and puddings sent in by friends of the prisoners.

From time to time we noticed that the Shinners would become rather boisterous in the evenings, singing, shouting, and carrying on. We discovered that this was due to the co-operation of Messrs. Libby and Co. who supplied the prisoners with tinned milk. Periodically a fair proportion of the tins were "inadvertently" filled with Jamieson's whisky! We turned a blind eye to this little caper as long as it didn't cause any trouble.

Early in 1922, when Lloyd George was Prime Minister, a scheme was evolved which it was hoped would finally settle the Irish question. Ireland was to be subdivided.

Six counties were to be ceded to the Protestant North under their own government, as the trouble then was mainly a religious one — Roman Catholic versus Protestant. The rest of the country was eventually to become the Republic of Ireland or Eire, and it was hoped that this would solve the problem forever. A forlorn hope as it has turned out.

With the partition came the release of the Ballakinler prisoners and the return of the British troops to England.

Great was the joy that day as nearly four thousand Sinn Feiners streamed out of the camp to catch their trains to all parts of Ireland. I think that we were nearly as pleased as they were to feel that our jailor duty was over.

When the camp finally closed I was due to return to Norwich, but was given a bit of leave before reporting for duty. We decided to go to Dublin, where my wife had been born and spent her childhood. Although my wife's family were "as Irish as the pigs," their religion was Church of Ireland and not Catholic. They were also pro-British and Royalists, which resulted in their having to leave Southern Ireland and lose their possessions.

While we were in Dublin an amusing sequel to Ballakinler occurred. My wife and I were walking down Clanbrassil Street in the early morning sunshine. I was in uniform. Suddenly coming towards us I noticed three enormous Irishmen wearing dark suits and looking rather sinister. I said to my wife: "I recognise these chaps; they were in Ballakinler camp. Unless you want to lose your husband I think we'd better get out of their way. They'll probably draw a gun on us."

My wife said: "Nonsense! They won't bear any malice. Let's just walk on."

So we walked on, and as we got abreast of them they recognised me and said in a most friendly way: "Sure and be Jebus it's that bastard from Ballakinler — come and have a glass of porter."

Off we went to the nearest pub and had a drink with them. A happy ending to my time in Ireland. After this short holiday we went back to Norwich where I rejoined my battery which had already arrived from Ireland. We settled down happily and looked forward to a long stay, but it was not to be.

The year was 1922 and we'd only been in Norwich a couple of months when I received a letter from the War Office informing me that I was to proceed to India on a four-year tour in September of that year. My wife was very bitter when I told her about this posting and said: "Are we never to have any peace?"

To which I replied: "This is what you get for marrying a soldier; it's just as well I'm not in the navy."

I was a bit fed up too as I didn't really want to go to India, so I went up to the War Office and saw an old friend of mine called Colonel Metcalfe. I'd served with him in World War I, and we called him "Lyddite Bill" as he favoured lyddite when shelling enemy positions. I turned on the sob stuff about being recently married and having just come back from Ireland and looking forward to a bit of peace.

The old boy looked at me and said: "Hodgson, you're bloody lucky. We're about to axe four hundred officers in the regiment and you've been selected to stay on. I can't think why! My advice to you is to pack your bags, go to India and thank your lucky stars you're not wearing a bowler hat."

So with my tail between my legs I left the War Office, and in due course embarked on the trooper S.S. Syria bound for India, where I was destined to spend twenty-five years — the happiest of my long army career.

9

Land of the five rivers

We embarked on S.S. Syria at Tilbury Docks and, sailing down the Thames and into the English Channel, started off on what was normally a three-week voyage via the Med and the Suez Canal.

When we reached the Red Sea it was fiendishly hot. For dinner we were all done up like Christmas trees in mess kit with stiff dress shirts and sweating like pigs. Suddenly a lovely cool breeze blew through the ship, and we realised that the captain had put the ship about. This was common practice when it was very hot, and usually lasted for about an hour. However, when the breeze continued for a couple of hours and we were still steaming north, we began to ask questions. We were told that we were to go back to Port Suez and await further orders.

At this time there was a lot of trouble in Turkey where a chap called Attaturk was chucking his weight about, and it looked as though Britain was going to become involved in it.

Having got to Port Suez we were supposed to disembark, but as there were not sufficient facilities for our disembarkation, we had to proceed back through the Suez Canal to Port Said. Here again facilities were not available, but apparently our ship was needed to take troops to Turkey. We were then ordered to go to Alexandria, and on arrival we were told what our role in the operation was to be.

We were to disembark, and with the troops on board, consisting of men from all branches of the army and air force, form ourselves into a composite battalion. We were then to relieve the British battalion stationed at Abbassia, near Cairo, who would then take over our ship and go to Turkey.

The families of officers and N.C.Os were to proceed to Cairo where the officers' families were to be accommodated at Shepheard's Hotel, and the N.C.Os' families elsewhere.

Unloading commenced and I took over command of some one hundred and fifty men who were to be formed into a company of infantry. My wife and other wives and families were transported to the station and put on the train for Cairo.

While forming my company, orders came: "Cancel everything — re-embark and resume voyage to India."

Realising that my wife was already on the train, and thinking that they might not have had the cancellation orders, I legged it as fast as I could to the station. Running down the platform I found my wife's carriage, and dragged her and the other occupants out. At that moment the train started with all the other wives and families on board, only to return a few hours later. I think my wife was rather disappointed — after all, Shepheard's was some pub!

We all re-embarked and went through the Suez Canal for the third time — surely a record for one voyage! Quite an uncanny experience was seeing the mirages on either side of the Canal. These usually took the form of an oasis consisting of palm trees and tents which faded away after a time. I never really understood the scientific explantion of this phenomenon, but I could fully understand the agonies of disappointment suffered by desert travellers.

Our first stop was Aden, where we went ashore and looked at the famous mermaid in the museum. It wasn't really my idea of a mermaid and looked more like an ugly fish. In actual fact it was a dugong. We also did a bit of sea bathing and I saw shark nets for the first time. The sharks were cruising up and down on the out-side, positively eyeing us in anticipation of a good meal. The sea at Aden was so buoyant that you simply couldn't sink, apparently owing to the high salt content.

After six weeks at sea, instead of the normal three, we arrived at Bombay and were told our ultimate destination, which was to be a place called Campbellpore in the Punjab, three days journey away by train. While on the long sea voyage I had tried to pick up a bit of the Hindustani (Urdu) language from a second-hand book I'd bought in London before leaving. I was assisted in my efforts by a colonel whom I discovered later was the chief examiner in languages at Army H.Q. in India. I was most gratified to find that when I tried a few words on the Indians in Bombay they actually understood.

During the voyage we had made friends with Major and Mrs. Stack, R.A.M.C., and by a strange coincidence they also had been posted to Campbellpore, where he was to be the senior medical officer. We managed to get a four-berth carriage which we shared with the Stacks, and this helped to alleviate what would otherwise have been a very dusty and rather monotonous journey.

The Indian trains were fairly comfortable because the gauge was very broad, and the catering and accommodation were good. Of course, being in this new world seething with humanity of all tribes and castes made the journey an education to us.

We stopped at most stations, and every one was teeming with people. Many were not passengers, but vendors of various types of food, which they sold to the appropriate caste. A familiar sound was from the purveyors of drinking water, who used to chant: *Hindu, Musalman, ki pani* (water), as they proceeded up and down the platform carrying their containers on each end of a bamboo pole which they balanced across their shoulders.

It was possible to buy practically anything in the way of food on the platform, and you could even have a haircut or a shave. We watched *chupaties* (a kind of pancake) being cooked over a charcoal fire for Muslims, and various other spicy delicacies which were all prepared on a "while you wait" basis. It was the accepted thing to have these fires going in open metal charcoal containers, called *sigeris,* all over the station platforms for the benefit of the third class passengers, who were not catered for on the train.

The average Indian passenger had no idea of timetables, and was happy to spend several days camping at the station, waiting for his train. They just dossed down on the platform with their bundles of bedding and clothing.

When the trains eventually arrived they were disgracefully over-crowded, with the passengers hanging on the outside and even sitting on the roof.

Feeling pretty travel worn and grubby, we finally arrived at the one-eyed little station that called itself Campbellpore, only to find that my unit hadn't been told we were coming, so no accommodation or transport had been arranged. Fortunately we were able to share the Stack's transport, but had to sleep in the *dak* bungalow for a few days.

These bungalows were run by the Indian Government and were located all over the country for the benefit of travellers. They were furnished and had the necessary staff to look after visitors, including a cook.

After six weeks at sea and three days on a train, it was rather discouraging to find, firstly, that we weren't expected, secondly, my unit had never heard of us, and thirdly, they didn't appear to care much anyway!

Not exactly an overwhelming welcome, but as I was only a lieutenant and as such was a very small pebble on a very large beach, we just had to lump it.

Luckily, the Stacks, who had a very nice bungalow, invited us to stay with them until our own was ready. We were most grateful.

The Punjab, which is now part of Pakistan, means the Land of the Five Rivers, which are the Indus, Jhelam, Ravi, Sutlej and Chenab. The latter four flow into the Indus, making it the largest river in Pakistan with its mouth at Karachi. The river Indus was to provide us with many happy hours of sport.

Campbellpore was one of many cantonments dotted about the North West Frontier of India, as it was called in those days. It was in the Punjab and the North West Frontier that the main portion of the Indian Army was located. This was mainly because we always feared an invasion from Russia.

The Army in India consisted of about three-quarters of Indian infantry and cavalry and a quarter British infantry, with some cavalry and artillery. All units were maintained at war strength. These cantonments were permanent military towns, situated some short distance from the principal cities, and were created after the Indian Mutiny. They were strategically designed with a view to preventing a similar uprising in the future.

Of course, as the servants were an integral part of our life in India, and, as no one servant would do two jobs, this necessitated having a large staff. It should be noted that at the time one rupee was worth one shilling and six pence. In order of importance the staff were as follows:

1. My bearer: He was in charge of the household, the other servants, and also acted as my valet. Salary — forty rupees a month;
2. The *Khansamah,* or cook — forty rupees;
3. The *Khitmagar,* or butler — twenty-five rupees;
4. The *Masalchi,* or washer up — twelve rupees;
5. The Sweeper, who cleaned the house and dealt with the primitive sanitary arrangements — ten rupees;
6. The *Bheesti,* or water carrier — ten rupees;
7. The *Mali,* or gardener — twelve rupees;
8. The *Dhobi,* or laundryman — twelve rupees;
9. The *Syce,* or groom. One had to have one *syce* for each horse, and as I had two horses, I had the same number of *syces* — eight rupees per *syce.*
10. The *Chowkidar,* or night watchman — ten rupees;
11. The *Punkawallah;* needed in the hot weather to pull the punka which made a breeze — ten rupees. There was no electricity then.
12. The *Ayah;* a personal maid or nanny.
13. In addition to this lot I was allotted a personal body guard, or orderly, in the form of an Indian *sepoy.* This was a relic of the Indian Mutiny days when one needed personal protection. He was provided free by the army.

Employing all these people cost us approximately 190 rupees a month, the rates of pay being laid down by the authorities. As my salary at that time was only three hundred rupees per month, the servant's salaries amounted to about two thirds of my own. The only redeeming feature was that they provided their own food and that ours was very cheap.

It might be thought that to employ all these servants was a ridiculous extravagance. I must explain that in those days in India we would have been ostracised by the Indians themselves, and would have lost face in their eyes if we hadn't employed servants and with the terrific over-population and poverty the British were looked upon as a source of employment.

However, as far as I, personally, was concerned I found this a pretty crippling form of charity! I had no other source of income apart from my pay, which was less in India than it had been in England. We struggled on for a few months, but it was pretty obvious that we weren't going to be able to keep our heads above water financially.

So, according to King's Regulations, which stipulate that if you are in financial difficulties you should report the fact to your commanding officer, I duly went to see the adjutant. Failing to do this and running into debt would have resulted in disciplinary action being taken against me. The adjutant was a Captain Freddy Morgan, who was a most helpful and understanding man.

Freddy Morgan later became Field Marshal Sir Frederick Morgan, and one of General Eisenhower's right-hand men. In fact, he planned the D-Day landings in France in World War II. He began this planning in 1941, setting up his secret H.Q. on the floors above a famous West End store. Towards the end General Morgan and his staff of two senior British officers and a band of young officers worked seven days a week, and gave up everything to do the job. It was accepted, practically without alteration, by Eisenhower and Montgomery. It represented three years of intensive work and is contained in a book the size of a family Bible.

"That's easy, tender your resignation and explain the circumstances, I'll draft the letter for you," said Freddy Morgan.

I was horrified at this suggestion.

"Oh, no," I replied, "I don't want to resign. Dammit, I'm hoping to make the army my career."

"Well," he said, "I don't think you'll have to resign, but let's try it, and if they do accept it, you can always withdraw it, or something like that."

Well, Freddy was a damn good chap on paper, and he drafted a

72

letter to the Commander-in-Chief in India, which I then signed. Of course, we had to wait some time for a reply, by the end of which I was a nervous wreck. One morning, Freddy sent for me and said there was a reply from the Commander-in-Chief. There was no question of my having to resign, and His Excellency had seen fit to increase my pay by 100 rupees a month. Of course we were overjoyed.

Shortly afterwards I had another lucky break as I was appointed station staff officer and cantonment magistrate, with third class judicial powers. This gave me an additional increase and brought my pay up to 500 rupees, and we were able to live a lot more comfortably.

Added to the increase in pay I had another windfall. My Colonel, Jim Scarlett, who was a bachelor, said to me one day: "I'd like to meet your wife and have a look at your bungalow." I naturally replied that we would be very pleased, and invited him for a drink.

During his visit he said: "You know, you want a bigger place than this."

"Well," I said, "this is what I've been allotted and it's all I can afford."

Then the colonel came up with the most amazing suggestion. He said that as a bachelor the bungalow allotted to him was far too big. He thought it would be a good idea if we exchanged bungalows. I told him I thought that would be marvellous, but that I couldn't possibly afford the rent of his place, which was for senior officers. The colonel then said that there was no question of that. He would continue to pay his rent and I would continue to pay mine.

My wife and I were absolutely overwhelmed by the colonel's generosity and we gratefully accepted his offer and moved into his bungalow. Such actions as these contributed so much to our happiness in Campbellpore, and it was an honour to serve under a commanding officer like Colonel Jim Scarlett.

One of the first requirements on arrival in India was to get a working knowledge of the lingua franca of the country, Hindustani. I have already mentioned that I bought a book in London which I had studied during the voyage. It wasn't obligatory for British Service officers in India to speak the language, but I felt that I would like to be able to communicate directly with my men, rather than through my Indian officer, who spoke perfect English.

I discussed the subject with my Indian officer, and asked him if he could produce a *munchi* (teacher) and he said that they had an excellent fellow called Jaffa Shah. He would arrange for him to come to my bungalow that afternoon.

At the appointed time I saw, coming up the drive, an elderly Indian with a long white beard, walking with a stick. He came up to the verandah where I was sitting, bowed from the waist and said: *"Salaams Sahib,* I am Jaffa Shah the *munchi."*

He was a charming old gentleman who had served with the Indian troops in France and spoke fluent French. We discussed the lessons and he then asked me if I had any books on the subject. So I trotted out my second-hand book I'd bought in London.

The old boy took the book from me, his face lit up and he beamed from ear to ear.

I said: "Is it any good?"

To which he replied with great pride: "Yes, I wrote it!"

Out of all the millions of people in India, what an incredible coincidence that I should meet the author of the book I'd bought in London. Our Hindustani lessons got off to a good start, and I soon acquired a working knowledge of the language.

In my unit I had an Indian officer called Suba Khan, a fine-looking Muslim chap to whom I took a liking straight away. He was a war-time officer and he told me that he was due to be retired quite soon. One day he surprised me by asking if he could become my bearer.

"Suba Khan", I said, "as an ex-Indian officer you surely can't want to take on a servant's job?"

He replied that as he lived in a village nearby he would like to take the job, and I was naturally delighted to have him. What a marvellous servant he turned out to be; nothing defeated him and nothing was too much trouble, as will be seen from an anecdote which I shall relate in the next chapter.

10

Bribery and abduction

I very much enjoyed the shooting opportunities that were available in the countryside round Campbellpore. Nowadays, since we have all become more enlightened and considerate towards wild life, I wouldn't dream of destroying these beautiful animals, but those were the days before so many species had become endangered and some culling was necessary. Even so, I used to feel a twinge of conscience whenever I saw my victim lying dead.

In the immediate vicinity of the cantonment there was plenty of partridge, snipe, quail and duck. These all provided good sport and good eating. One of our cook's specialities was to roast a quail inside an orange which gave it a delicious flavour.

After a few shooting expeditions with brother officers, I decided to launch out on my own and have a go at shooting chinkara, which were found in the low hills some five miles from Campbellpore. This antelope is a small two-horned goat-like animal, very elusive and difficult to bag.

My main problem was transport. In those days I had only a push-bike and a horse, both unsuitable for carting all the shooting and camping impedimenta. Luckily my wife had a governess-cart drawn by a twelve-hand high white pony, known as Tum Tum Tommy. I had no choice but to use this to transport myself, Suba Khan and all the equipment.

In order to reach the shooting area we had to cross a river. Normally this would have been no problem, but on this occasion when we arrived at the river we found it was in spate.

I said to Suba Khan: "Well, we obviously can't get this lot across the river, we'll have to go back to cantonments and try another day."

Old Suba Khan replied in Hindustani: *Tak hai Sahib hum bundabust karengi,* meaning, "Don't worry, Sahib, I'll arrange everything."

I felt that it was quite impossible and highly dangerous to attempt it, but Suba Khan was so confident that I decided to let him have a go.

He stripped and proceeded to swim across the river and then disappeared into a village on the other side. Some time later he reappeared leading a ruddy camel, escorted by some of the villagers. Into the river plunged old Suba Khan and a rather reluctant camel, and swam across to my side. I'd never before seen a camel swimming and didn't realise that they could. In due course they landed on my side of the river and climbed up the bank to where the pony and I were waiting.

"What's the camel for Suba Khan?" I asked.

"You're going to ride it across the river, Sahib," he replied.

"That will be the day," I said — or the equivalent in Hindustani. "I've never ridden a camel before, and how do you know he'll be happy with me on board?"

Suba Khan made suitable noises, brought the camel to its knees, and with considerable misgivings, but not wishing to let down the British Raj, I stepped on board, clutching my rifle, "binos" and camera. Suba Khan then made another sort of noise, whereupon the camel lurched to its feet with much grunting and other camel noises. The huge animal then turned to look at me with the most supercilious expression on its face, which rather indicated that he knew I was just a bungling amateur in the camel-riding world.

Suba Khan then led the camel down to the water's edge, and, after offering a quick prayer to Allah, who seemed to be the most appropriate deity to appeal to on this particular occasion, we embarked on what I regarded as a most dangerous crossing. With the river washing round my feet and Suba Khan swimming ahead, still leading the camel by a rope tied round his waist, we eventually landed on the other side.

Suba Khan then made camel noises in reverse and the old *oont* (Hindustani for camel) got into a semi-recumbent posture so that I could dismount. From his expression I thought that his relief was as great as mine.

My intrepid bearer then announced that he was going to swim back and fetch my bedding, and other items which were still in the cart on the other side under the care of one of the villagers. He made two crossings and brought all my equipment over safely on his head.

Then came the most difficult part of the whole operation. Suba Khan announced that he was going back to get Tum Tum Tommy and the trap. I thought it was virtually impossible to get that tiny pony and cart across the raging torrent, but Suba Khan never wavered in his determination, so I decided not to interfere and to let him get on with it.

Watching anxiously from the bank, I saw Suba Khan leading Tum Tum Tommy down to the water's edge, and in due course inducing him into the river with the cart still attached. As they reached the deep water the pony became more and more submerged, until only his nose and ears were visible, and the cart was completely awash and practically under water.

Suba Khan's head was just visible as he swam ahead still leading the pony, with the villager bringing up the rear. I was terrified that the weight of the water in the cart would cause them to be swept away downstream. However, they gradually got across and appeared to be none the worse for the struggle. We dried Tum Tum, gave him some food, reloaded the cart and made for the *dak* bungalow some miles away.

By this time the whole village had turned out, and they gave us a great send-off, accompanied by shouts of *Shabash, Sahib, Shabash* (Well done Sahib). All the credit was due to the enterprise and courage of Suba Khan. No praise would be too high for him.

We spent the night in the dak bungalow where Suba Khan produced an adequate meal and we both slept like logs for about twelve hours. Next morning, with a *shikari* (hunter) from the village, I bagged a chinkara with quite a good head. We ate the meat, which was rather strong, and preserved the skin and head. Later that day, we started back for Campbellpore and, to my great relief, found that the river had subsided and we were able to recross it without much difficulty.

During my tenure as cantonment magistrate I had several interesting experiences. One of these concerned a wealthy Indian who had died in the cantonments and therefore came under my jurisdiction.

Certain legal documents had to be signed in connection with his children's inheritance, so I went along to the house one day accompanied by my Sikh ex-subadar-major, who was my head clerk, and who rather looked down on Muslims.

We were invited into one of the palatial rooms and presently the son of the deceased was brought in. I identified him as best I could and he and I then signed the papers. That was a piece of cake and the real problem was still to come — his sister. She came along escorted by a couple of Muslim women, all wearing *bourkhas*. The only visible part of their faces was their eyes looking out of a sort of trellis work. As the girl came up to the table to sign the documents I explained to the women that I couldn't let her sign unless I positively identified her, which would mean removing the *bourkha*. This really put the cat among the canaries: "Oh! Sahib, it is not the custom for any stranger to look on the face of a Muslim woman, particularly an unmarried girl," one of the women replied.

I turned to my Sikh clerk and said: "What do we do about this?"

The Sikh, who had little regard for Muslim customs, replied: "You must see her face before you sign the document."

I explained to the women that unless they were prepared to let me see the girl I wouldn't be justified in signing the papers. Thinking that perhaps it was the presence of a Sikh that was causing the trouble, I suggested that my clerk left the room so that I would be the only stranger present. This still didn't placate the women, and eventually they withdrew and an elderly male member of the family intervened and asked if I wouldn't make an exception in this case.

I told him I was sorry but I couldn't help. I had been endowed with certain powers which I musn't abuse. Either they must produce the girl minus *bourkha* and we would get on with the business, or we must forget the whole thing.

After some time the girl re-appeared with the two women, but without her *bourkha*. She came forward without any sign of embarrassment, smiling and appearing to be quite happy about the whole situation. I spoke to her in Hindustani and made my apologies to her. She said that it was quite all right, and we got on with the legal business without further ado.

I think that the Muslim heiress really quite enjoyed the whole episode, probably because being of the younger generation she was more emancipated than the older women. It certainly taught me quite a lot about India and its customs.

Another episode during my period as cantonment magistrate concerned a Hindu called Lalta Pershad, who was contractor to the cantonment and a very wealthy man.

One afternoon I was going out to play tennis and as I was leaving the bungalow an Indian carrying a huge basket of fruit arrived.

"Who is this for?" I asked.

"It's for you, Sahib, from Lalta Pershad," the man replied. I put my hand on the basket of fruit, which was the Indian way of acknowledging a gift, and called my bearer Suba Khan. He came along and took the basket away and I pushed off to tennis.

When I got back to the bungalow I had to change into my mess kit as I was dining in the mess that night. I'd had a bath and was partially dressed, with Suba Khan in attendance. I noticed that he kept fidgeting, and obviously had something on his mind. So I asked him: "What's the matter with you, Suba Khan?"

"Oh! Sahib, you haven't looked at the letter that came with the fruit," he said.

He handed me the letter. I opened it, and to my astonishment found three hundred rupee notes inside — as much as my month's pay. I realised this was a bribe of some sort, for what reason I was not aware, so as soon as I was dressed I walked over to the colonel's bungalow to ask his advice. He suggested that I left the money with him and that we would deal with the matter in the morning in my office.

The following morning the colonel came round and said: "It's entirely up to you what you do about this matter, but as you are fairly new to this country I'm going to suggest the following: we will keep the three hundred rupees and donate it to the Indian Military Hospital. Get a receipt and send it to Lalta Pershad with our thanks. As to Lalta Pershad, obviously he is trying to bribe you, and this is a very serious offence, especially in the case of a man of his calibre and in his position. Under the Cantonment Act you can declare Lalta an undesirable person, and as such he will be ordered to leave within thirty days."

I said to the colonel: "Don't you think this punishment is too severe, as he is an Indian and our contractor?"

"Well," he replied, "I think that's what you should do."

Obviously it was very difficult for me to go against the colonel's wishes, particularly as he was so much more experienced in Indian affairs and I had a high regard for his opinion.

I sent the money to the hospital, got a receipt, and wrote a letter to Lalta Pershad declaring him an undesirable person and telling him that he had to vacate the cantonment within thirty days.

Within a few days he came to my office and literally got on his hands and knees and implored me to take a more lenient view of the affair.

I told him that the colonel and I had discussed the matter and that he, as Officer Commanding the Station, had instructed me as to what action to take. I also told him that I thought he had been very stupid to try and bribe me and that nothing further could be done.

"But Sahib, it's the custom," he said.

"I'm sorry, but it's not our custom, and there the matter must end," I told him.

So Lalta packed his bags and eventually left the cantonment. I couldn't help feeling sorry for the chap, because as he had pointed out, according to Indian custom he had done no wrong, and as I was to discover later, bribery and corruption were a way of life in India.

Whilst in Campbellpore we had a dramatic incident in which a "gentleman" called Ajib Khan was involved. He was a Pathan, and a notorious character who lived in tribal territory in the North West Frontier. He had committed some offence which had incurred the displeasure of the Indian Government, and in retaliation they had deprived him of his permit to enter India. This meant that he couldn't come into India legally and had to remain in tribal territory.

Ajib Khan was determined to make the Indian government rescind their embargo, and to this end he and some of his followers came into India one night and abducted an English girl from a cantonment called Kohat and murdered her mother, who was trying to defend her. The daughter's name was Molly Ellis, and her father was a Colonel Ellis in the Indian Army. She was about seventeen at the time.

They took her away into tribal territory and Ajib Khan then issued an ultimatum to the Indian Government saying that unless his permit was restored he would not be responsible for the life of Molly Ellis. The Government agreed to his terms and it was arranged that a small party of unarmed Indian sepoys would be sent into tribal territory to bring the girl back. Mrs. Starr, a doctor at the mission hospital, courageously volunteered to accompany the party. After much discussion the Indian Government reluctantly agreed to let Mrs. Starr go, and the party proceeded into tribal territory, where they found Molly Ellis unharmed, and brought her back to Kohat.

Mrs. Starr, who eventually became Mrs. Underhill, was awarded the Gold Kaiser-I-Hind medal for her bravery in the rescue operation.

However, this was not the end of the incident, because as far as I remember the Indian Government went back on its word regarding the permit for Ajib Khan. This, of course, infuriated him, and he threatened to abduct further white women from any cantonment between Peshawar and Delhi.

Campbellpore was situated within walking distance of the North West Frontier where Ajib Khan was domiciled, and was therefore one of the most vulnerable stations. Experience had shown that his threat had to be regarded seriously, so immediate steps were taken to protect the women in the cantonment.

Alarm systems were set up, one of these being the firing of an eighteen-pounder gun which could be heard all over the station.

Unfortunately I had to be away during this period as I was range officer at a place called Akora, some fifty miles away on the other side of the Indus. I could only get back at weekends, so during the week my wife had to have an Indian armed guard at the bungalow consisting of one N.C.O. and three men. They used to come on guard at dusk and camp on the verandah until dawn the next morning. My wife found them a bit of a nuisance as they talked and rattled their cooking pots most of the night, but as I pointed out to her, it was preferable to being abducted.

Some time later, after I had come back from Akora, we decided to have a big dance for officers, N.C.Os and their wives. It was to be held in one of the large barrack rooms. The Ajib Khan "scare" was still on, although we hadn't been raided up to that point, but all officers and N.C.Os were still carrying revolvers on and off duty. The dance was in full swing when suddenly the eighteen-pounder started to boom. The dancing came to an abrupt end as the officers and N.C.Os went to their action stations, and all the women were locked in the barrack room under guard.

Shortly afterwards it was reported that figures had been seen moving towards the cantonment. Fire was opened, and it was only then discovered that what had been taken for crouching figures were in fact jackals on their nightly scavenging expedition.

Of course, as a result of our jackal debacle our brigade became the laughing stock of the district, and it took quite a bit of living down.

Ajib Khan did eventually make a proper raid on Campbellpore and this was taken care of by the Indian Police who were responsible as it was part of their normal duties. I gather that he was either killed or captured, and that was the end of this saga.

11

"Grey Dawn" and a duck shoot

I have already mentioned Akora where we had an artillery practice camp. As range officer I was responsible for the placing and observation of targets, and the general running of the range. I spent about three months there under canvas and found the job very interesting.

The administrative part of the camp was separated from the rest by means of two belts of barbed wire, primarily to protect us from the attentions of the notorious dacoits. They were a band of nomadic professional robbers who lived by thieving of all kinds, specialising in rifles which they could sell at a great profit to the Pathan, Mashud and Afridi tribesmen with whom we were constantly at war, although, strangely enough, we used to recruit them into the Indian Army.

The dacoits had the most amazing ability to carry out their nefarious activities, and wouldn't hesitate to kill anybody who got in their way. They were a menace right along the Frontier and well into the Punjab. We had to take extraordinary precautions to prevent the theft of arms, particularly rifles, and the penalty for losing a rifle was very severe. Our sentries occasionally had to have their rifles chained to them when they were on duty, and the dacoits would even kill them in order to get the weapons.

We were losing quite a lot of stuff out of the camp, even large rolled-up tents. How they got them over the belts of barbed wire right under the noses of the sentries was a mystery to us.

One evening I was dining with a brigade that had come up to do their annual artillery practice. I was talking to the colonel, who was on his first visit to Akora and had recently come out to India. I was telling him about the dacoits and their habits and said: "You know they can even get into your tent, take all the sheets, pillows and blankets off your bed and you won't wake up."

"Oh, rubbish!" he said. "If it happened to me I'd certainly wake up."

I replied: "Well, I can assure you that it's happened, so watch out!"

A week later I met the same colonel and he hailed me and said: "How right you were about the dacoits. Last night one of them got into my tent, pinched all my bedding and I never woke or felt a thing. I still can't believe it. I think I must have been doped."

I was to have a pretty shattering experience myself a few days later. I was sharing a very large tent with our medical officer, a chap called Yardley Ecutt. He slept at one end and I at the other. The M.O. had a habit of sleeping with a candle, shaded by an open book, burning next to his bed.

I was lying in bed and for some reason couldn't get off to sleep. I could hear the sentries moving up and down outside. Suddenly I noticed that the roof of the tent was flapping, and as there was no wind I couldn't understand what was causing it. I was soon to find out.

Luckily there was enough light from Yardley Ecutt's candle to show up the interior of the tent. I realised that something was wrong, and managed to look round without moving my head. There, having just crept under the wall of the tent, was one of these dacoits. He was greased all over and naked apart from a loin cloth. Even in the poor light I could see that he was carrying a dagger between his teeth. As we were always armed at Akora, I had my revolver strapped to my thigh.

I debated as to how I should deal with this situation. By this time I had my hand on the butt of the revolver, and thought I might be able to shoot him through the blankets. However, I then realised that as I was sleeping under four blankets it would be impossible to shoot the dacoit as the bullet would be unlikely to penetrate them and do any good. If I'd pulled the revolver from under the blanket he'd have been off like a scalded cat, and with the sentries at such close quarters, I might even have hit one of them.

In the circumstances I decided the only thing I could do was to let out a blood-curdling yell: "Dacoit, dacoit!"

The alarm was immediately given, but by this time he had bolted and despite all our efforts we never got him.

Living in a village near Akora was a *lambadar* or village head-man, and as such he had the title of Khan Sahib. He had been given the contract of clearing the range of all dud shells and broken metal. He then resold it to the Government as scrap.

Khan Sahib had to provide the labour force for this job, and he and I had to work in close co-operation. Every morning we would ride out to the range together and I would indicate the area where the shelling would take place.

One morning the Khan Sahib appeared on a lovely grey Arab pony, which I admired very much, and I said to him: "Would you consider selling that pony?"

"Oh no, Sahib, I would never sell her. I have just bought her and she suits my needs."

"Well," I said, "if you ever change your mind let me know." So I more or less abandoned the idea of owning the grey pony. Then one morning on the range there was a terrific explosion. I was back in the camp at the time when the Khan Sahib came riding in on the grey pony. He was in a state of great agitation and told me there had been an accident on the range and that eight of his men had been killed and a number injured.

Contrary to their instructions they had been fiddling about with a dud shell, instead of waiting until our chaps had blown it up. They had been trying to knock off the fuse and had caused it to detonate, with disastrous results.

"Well, now, of course, I must have money quickly," Khan Sahib told me," as I must compensate the relatives of the men who have been killed. Unfortunately, I will have to sell my grey pony. Do you still want her?"

I told him that I would be delighted to buy her, and we settled on a price of six hundred rupees, a fair amount for a hack in those days. I realised that she had the makings of a first class polo pony. Thus I became the owner of this beautiful mare that I christened Grey Dawn.

Once again my resourceful bearer Suba Khan came to the rescue and volunteered to ride my charger Rufus and lead Grey Dawn back to Campbellpore, as I had to travel by train. Once back there I got down to training Grey Dawn as a polo pony. She was perfect. I spent a lot of time with her and she had just the right temperament for polo.

There was an interesting sequel to the Grey Dawn story. Subsequently I was appointed staff captain at Abbottabad, a Gurkha station up in the hills some seventy miles from Campbellpore. I played polo there quite frequently on Grey Dawn. One day I had just come off the ground after playing a chukka, when a very smart-looking Sikh captain approached me.

"I'm Captain Singh, Aide-de-Camp to His Highness the Maharajah of Patiala," he said. "His Highness has been watching you on the grey pony and he would like to buy it. Would you consider selling her?"

"Yes," I said, "at a price. I don't want to sell her, but if I did, I would want ten thousand rupees." I realised that this was a fantastic price, the equivalent of about seven hundred and fifty pounds sterling, but I would only sell Grey Dawn in order to get the money to buy other ponies, which I used to train and then re-sell.

"All right, I'll tell His Highness," replied Captain Singh. I thought I'd priced myself out of the market, but about an hour later Captain Singh returned and said that His Highness thought the price was too high. He was willing to pay eight thousand rupees.

I replied that I realised the price was high, but that unless I could get it I didn't want to sell. Of course I knew that ten thousand rupees to the Maharajah of Patiala was a mere drop in the ocean, and I was gambling on this.

Well, after a little more discussion he agreed to the price and Grey Dawn became the property of His Highness.

Although I was very sorry to lose her, it was the best deal I ever did as a "gentleman horse-coper," and enabled me to buy several other ponies.

As I mentioned before, there was excellent duck shooting in the vicinity of Campbellpore.

On one occasion I was invited by a *lambadar* (headman of the village) to go on a duck shoot with him and some of his Indian friends. I spent the night in a *dak* bungalow as the shoot was to start very early. The next morning I joined the party at his village and we set off — there were about twelve guns.

At this time, I hadn't done much duck shooting in India, so was very interested to see what the drill was.

We started walking towards some *jheels* (lakes) when I noticed that one of the party was carrying a hooded falcon. So I said to the *lambadar:* "What's that in aid of?"

"You'll see," he replied.

Cautiously we approached one of these huge *jheels,* which was covered with duck. There must have been several hundred of them. As we got fairly near, the chap with the falcon took off its hood and let the bird go. We waited a short time and then the *lambadar* said: *Accha, argie jow!* (All right, go ahead.)

We walked forward and got so close to the duck that we could almost touch them. Although the birds were obviously agitated they made no attempt to fly off.

"What's keeping the birds on the water?" I asked the *lambadar.* The old boy just pointed up into the sky, and there was the falcon hovering over the *jheel* and controlling all these hundreds of duck. I'd never seen anything like it.

Suddenly the falcon swooped and grabbed a duck that was close to me at the edge of the *jheel,* dragged it on to dry ground and killed it. At the same time as the falcon struck the duck, the rest of the flock started to leave the water in a huge cloud.

At this moment all the guns, except mine, opened fire, with the duck barely off the water. When the bombardment ceased and birds had gone I turned to the *lambadar* and said: "This is sheer slaughter — it's not my idea of duck shooting. The birds haven't got a sporting chance. Are we shooting for the pot or for sport?"

Incidentally, between the eleven guns they had killed about fifty birds.

The *lambadar* asked me what I suggested, and I told him that I thought the birds should be given a fair chance.

"All right," he replied, "We'll go on to the next *jheel* and when you open fire we'll follow suit."

We walked on and came to another *jheel*, also covered with duck, presumably the ones we had chased from the previous place. The same procedure was carried out up to the point when the duck started leaving the water. I was standing with my gun at the ready. When I thought the duck had a reasonable chance I opened fire, missed with the first barrel, and got a duck with the second. There were several other guns firing, but when we totted it up, our casualty rate had fallen to five. The other guns thought this was a dud show and a waste of ammunition.

However, I stuck to my "sporting chance" principle, to which they agreed with some reluctance, and even so we bagged quite a number of duck during the morning.

After concluding the duck shoot we decided to have a go at snipe. This was a different kettle of fish! Snipe are not an easy shot at the best of times, and we only managed to bag a dozen. We then decided to call it a day and started back for the *lambadar's* village, where we were to have lunch.

As we walked along the bank of the Sutlej river I spotted a Brahminee duck flying very high. I thought it was well out of range of a twelve-bore gun and said to the *lambadar:* "I bet you five rupees you can't bring that one down." Anyway, he upped with his gun, and to my amazement brought the duck out of the sky. My opinion of him as a shot rose considerably. The *lambadar* then said to me: "Have you ever noticed the way Brahminee duck always sit on opposite sides of the river and call to one another?"

I replied that I had indeed noticed this.

"Well," he said, "according to Hindu legend they are the rein-carnation of a Hindu boy and girl. These two young people fell in love but were not allowed to marry as their families were of different castes. The lovers were so heart-broken that they decided to commit suicide by drowning themselves in a river. Ever since, in their reincarnated state, they have been calling to each other across the river."

Needless to say, after that I couldn't bring myself to shoot a Brahminee duck! I felt that I should be separating the lovers again.

We eventually reached the village, and just before we got to the house I noticed a white woman dressed in Indian costume working with Indian women in a field. So I said to the old *lambadar:* "What on earth is a white woman doing here?"

"Oh, she's the wife of one of the villagers. He went over to France during the war with the Indian Expeditionary Force, married a French woman and brought her back here."

I suggested that I might talk to her and find out how she had settled down in India, but he didn't think it would be a good idea, so I left it. However, I did mention it to the Superintendent of Police in Campbellpore, as white women who were married to Indians frequently disappeared. Usually they died from swallowing ground glass, which was mixed with their food, and administered by the other wives out of jealousy. This part of India was predominantly Muslim and a man could have any number of wives. One rich merchant in Rawalpindi had a hundred — poor devil!

As we walked along to the *lambadar's* house we got onto the subject of the *purdah* system. Being new to India I was interested to learn more about their customs. I said to him: "Why do you keep your women in *purdah?"*

"Well," he said, "it's an Indian custom, of course, and I think it's a good one. At least I know what my wives are doing now — they're in *purdah* in their *zenana.* I bet you don't know what your wife's doing in Campbellpore!"

I laughed and replied: "You've got a point there!"

When the party arrived at his house we were shown into a large room with a long low table in the centre, beautifully decorated with flowers. There were rugs on the floor on which we sat. No women were present and I was the only white person among about fifteen Indians. Servants came, removed our shoes, and washed our hands and feet.

We nibbled little snacks called samoosas while the main course was being served. This was a delicious chicken pilau, a traditional Muslim dish containing rice and many spices. Of course there were no knives and forks, and one had to be very careful to adhere to the custom of eating with the fingers of one's left hand. To have used the right hand would have horrified the Muslims who use their right hands for other purposes.

Luckily I had been put wise on this point so didn't disgrace myself.

Well, having consumed this enormous repast which was washed down with quantities of sickly sweet fruit drinks, I rose to my feet with some difficulty, thanked my host for his hospitality, and returned to Campbellpore on a buckboard which I had borrowed for the trip.

These buckboards were used extensively as transport at that time in India. They were two-wheeled vehicles drawn by one horse, and had the absolute minimum of everything, including comfort. The chief advantage was their mobility and the fact that you could take them over practically any terrain.

I arrived back at the bungalow with my spoils and was effusively welcomed by my wife. However, when I kissed her she recoiled with an expression of disgust and revulsion on her face.

"What on earth's the matter?" I said, feeling rather taken aback.

"It's your breath," she replied. "You absolutely reek of garlic." Then I remembered the chicken *pilau* and the Indians' love of garlic flavouring. We had to sleep back-to-back for the next two nights.

12

Quakes, plague and rabies

My duties as cantonment magistrate were certainly varied. One day I received a message from the Sudar Bazaar, the civilian part of the cantonment where the Indian trades-people lived, to say that there was an outbreak of plague. I didn't realise at the time what the implications were, but I was soon to learn.

I immediately contacted our young medical officer, Captain Carter, R.A.M.C., who had also recently arrived from the United Kingdom. He was about six foot four inches tall and as thin as a pencil. He came round and we went down to the Bazaar together. We started investigating, and were then tipped off about a certain house suspected of harbouring a case of plague. We knocked at the door and an Indian opened it.

"We'd like to have a look around your house," I said.

He replied: *Acha Sahib, under au* (all right Sir, come in.)

We looked round the house and everything seemed to be in order. Then we came to a room and found it locked. I asked the owner to open the door, and he answered that there was only rubbish in the room, he hadn't used it for ages, and that in any case he'd lost the key.

I told him that unless he found the key jolly quickly we'd have to break down the door. Off he went and within a few minutes had found the key. From the start I had been suspicious, and when I opened the door my suspicions were confirmed.

The Doc and I went inside and there, lying on a bed, was an Indian woman in the last throes of plague. All her glands were swollen, she looked ghastly and was obviously dying.

Well, it was now over to the Doc to take the necessary action. One of the first things to be done was to evacuate the Sudar Bazaar and get the population into a temporary village, which we had to build. The huts were made of bamboo and straw, as subsequently they had to be burnt. In the meantime, their permanent homes in the Sudar Bazaar had to be fumigated and the plague-carrying rats destroyed.

The Doc and I got out of the Bazaar as fast as we could. On arrival at the drive leading to my bungalow I stripped to the buff, in case I was carrying any of the plague-infected fleas from the rats. I left my clothes at the gate and strolled nonchalantly up to the bungalow in full view of the servants. Once inside I had a bath in Dettol and just hoped for the best. All the clothes I had been wearing were burnt but I was able to claim on expenses for the cost of a new outfit.

In our part of the Punjab, on the border of the North West Frontier, earthquakes occurred pretty frequently. These varied in intensity from a mild tremor to a severe 'quake, such as the one in Quetta in 1935 when thirty-five thousand people, both army personnel and Baluchis, were killed or injured.

One evening we were sitting on our verandah enjoying a pre-dinner drink. Suddenly a loud rumbling noise accompanied by a strong wind started. The trees began to sway and the birds made a commotion, having been shaken out of their roosting places. We ran out into the open until it had subsided.

This was our first experience of an earthquake, but as it was over quickly we weren't unduly perturbed. We eventually had dinner and went to bed.

In the middle of the night the 'quake started again, and suddenly there was the most terrific crash accompanied by falling masonry and dust. It was pitch black and there was no electricity in those days. We groped around and eventually found a candle, and by its light were able to see the cause of the noise. The wall which divided our bedroom from the living room had completely collapsed. Luckily it had fallen into the sitting room and not into the bedroom. Had it fallen the other way I would not have been telling this story today.

Needless to say we didn't have any sleep for the rest of that night. Although in later years we were to experience much worse 'quakes, we were never closer to death than we were that night.

Early one morning I was to go on a special parade, at which the colonel was to be present. I was done up like the proverbial Christmas tree and was waiting for the *syce* (groom) to bring my horse. She was the first horse that I owned in India and was very excitable, restive and difficult to mount. I said to the *syce:* "Be careful and don't let go until I tell you."

Just as I got my left foot into the stirrup, the horse, which had been prancing around the whole time, suddenly reared and knocked the syce down. He naturally let go. of the reins, and off she galloped with me standing up in the stirrup on the near side. As much as I tried, I couldn't get my right leg over and my seat into the saddle. The high back arch of the regimental saddle added to my difficulties. The horse kept on bucking and jumping down the road, and then suddenly swerved to the right. I came unstuck and fell into a bush in which, unfortunately, was a concrete pillar.

I felt as though I had broken my back and every other bone in my body. However, I managed to stagger to my feet and crept back to the bungalow. By this time the *syce* had caught the horse and was waiting for me to remount. She had quietened down a bit by then, but I said to the *syce:* "I don't think I can possibly make it."

He said: "Sahib, you must try."

So with the assistance of two *syces* and a mounting block I managed to get into the saddle, in absolute agony. And in a somewhat dishevelled state I appeared on the parade ground.

There I found the whole regiment on parade, with the colonel mounted on his horse in front. Being late I rode up to the C.O., saluted, and made my apologies, saying that I'd been thrown from my horse. He just looked at me and in an icily sarcastic voice said: "Why don't you learn how to ride?"

What bigger insult could be offered to a Weedon-trained riding instructor!

Anyway, I joined my battery and after a short time I just couldn't sit in the saddle. So I rode up to the C.O. again and said that I was in hellish pain and could I be excused. This time the old boy was most sympathetic — he realised that I wasn't pulling a fast one. He got me into hospital, where I was examined, and did everything he could to help. I hadn't broken any bones, but my spine was very badly bruised, and for years afterwards I suffered from backache and lumbago.

Another occupational hazard with which we had to contend was frequent outbreaks of rabies. There was no vaccine for general anti-rabic treatment as there is today, so our dogs had to be guarded very carefully and never left the garden without us. Affected dogs were usually found in the Indian area and were destroyed whenever possible.

My wife was out riding one day and was going through an Indian village when a pariah dog rushed out and jumped up, biting her horse on the hindquarters and drawing quite a lot of blood. They returned to the cantonments and the horse was put into his stable, and some time later developed rabies and died. Luckily the dog hadn't bitten my wife's leg, which it might well have done.

While still in Campbellpore we had an outbreak amongst the dogs in the cantonment belonging to our military families. One suspected case was sent down to our vet for examination, and was declared rabid and destroyed. This vet had a habit whenever he was examining an animal. He had a little moustache which he used to stroke with the forefinger of his right hand. It was just an unconscious movement while he was thinking.

A couple of days after examining this rabid dog the vet went on leave to England. During the voyage the poor devil contracted rabies. Of course the authorities on the ship were in no position to deal with the disease and in due course he died at sea — a most ghastly death. We could only presume that he had contracted the disease through fingering his moustache while examining the dog.

Whenever it was suspected that you had been in contact with a rabid animal you were immediately sent to the only centre in

India for anti-rabic treatment, a place called Kasauli, near Simla. There you would undergo the necessary treatment which was usually successful. The only snag was that if you were a long distance from Kasauli the chances were that you might develop the disease before you got there. Distances in India were so great and transport was comparatively slow. There were no such things as planes to cope with this sort of an emergency.

After some eighteen months in Campbellpore I had another stroke of luck. We were having our annual inspection by the brigade commander from Abbottabad, Brigadier Cunningham, a very much decorated senior officer. He was accompanied by his brigade major, an officer named Nigel Wilson.

At the conclusion of the inspection we returned to my office and to my surprise the brigadier turned to me and said: "You're doing a very good job here, Hodgson, I'm very pleased with what I've seen today. Would you like to come to Abbottabad as my staff captain?"

"Yes Sir," I replied, "I'd like that very much."

He then told me that the pay would be very much better and that it would be an interesting job. In fact, when he told me what the increase would be I said: "Don't worry to arrange transport Sir, I'll walk!"

The pay was, in fact, one thousand and four hundred rupees, more than twice what I was getting at Campbellpore.

So we packed our bags and off we went to Abbottabad, some seventy miles away. It was a semi-hill station and the climate and living conditions were much better than in Campbellpore.

The station consisted mainly of Gurkha regiments — the First and Second Battalions of the Fifth Regiment and the First and Second Battalions of the Sixth Regiment. Also stationed there were a regiment of mountain artillery, and the Thirteenth Frontier Force depot. It was a new experience for me, being British Service, as all the other units were Indian Army.

I got to know the Gurkhas pretty well and admired them very much for their high standard of discipline and efficiency. The officers and men were so dedicated. The Gurkhas were recruited from Nepal, a very isolated and mountainous state in the Himalayas. They were Mongolian-looking in appearance, Hindu by religion and their language was Nepali. The traditional Gurkha weapon is the *kukhri,* a very broad-bladed sharp knife which they always carried, as it formed part of their equipment.

The Gurkha brigades were known as the Guards of the Indian Army, a tribute which I think they richly deserved. They were used primarily on the Frontier, where we were constantly at war with the tribesmen. Gurkhas were also frequently used on the plains when British troops were in the hills during the hot weather and therefore not available. They were most useful for quelling communal riots, which were a frequent occurrence, because, like the British troops, they were impartial. In some ways they were more suitable than the British troops, being indigenous to the country.

The Gurkha's reputation for bravery is renowned world-wide. They won the most incredible number of V.C.s in both world wars. Their complete disregard for danger is well-illustrated by the following true story.

A certain Colonel Gough of a Gurkha regiment was training a newly formed parachute regiment in their duties. When it came to the day when they were going to make their first jump the senior Gurkha officer turned to Colonel Gough and said. "Please Sir, the first time we jump, may we have parachutes?"

It was while at Abbottabad that I met for the first time a Gurkha officer by the name of Colonel Bill Slim of the Sixth Gurkhas. He was later to become Field Marshal Sir William Slim, one of the most outstanding generals of World War II, and afterwards Governor-General of Australia. During our first acquaintance when he was a Brevet Lieutenant Colonel I realised that he was destined for high places, and during my time in India our paths crossed several times, resulting in some amusing incidents.

Earthquakes were more common at Abbottabad than at my previous station, in fact we used to get one practically every day. They were noisy, but usually pretty mild. Most of the buildings were constructed to meet these conditions, being made of wood and plaster.

One evening my wife and I were invited to dinner with a young couple called Cunningham. He was a captain in the Thirteenth Frontier Force and, incidentally, won the V.C. in Malaya during World War II.

The Cunninghams lived in a double-storey house and had a small child, who was upstairs asleep. In the middle of dinner a 'quake started, rather more severely than usual as the building started to rock. Mrs. Cunningham was worried about her child and rushed upstairs to see if she was all right. She was away for such a long time that we became concerned. Then we heard banging and Mrs. Cunningham's voice calling for help, so we went outside and shouted up to the bedroom window.

Mrs. Cunningham put her head out and said that the door had jammed and she couldn't get out. Despite all our efforts we couldn't open it from our side either, as the force of the 'quake had completely jammed it. Worried about the possibility of further tremors, we eventually decided that the quickest way to rescue Mrs. Cunningham and the child was by way of a rope made of sheets knotted together. Luckily there were enough sheets in the bedroom, so with her dinner guests standing down below, our hostess, in long evening dress, with her baby in her arms, managed to clamber down the improvised rope to safety. We all cheered and the baby didn't even wake up through it all.

These were the sort of interludes that one came to accept as part of social life in Abbottabad.

As staff captain, I used to share Sunday duties with the brigade major. Someone had to be available to deal with urgent correspondence, and other matters.

On one occasion I was at the table opening letters while the Gurkha orderly watched from the doorway. Suddenly I heard a loud rumbling noise, like an express train approaching, and realised it was a 'quake coming. Having experienced so many I was rather inclined to ignore it, and just carried on with my job.

Without warning there was a deafening crash right overhead. I leapt out of my seat and made a dash for the door. My Gurkha orderly, seeing that I was clearing out, decided to do the same, and we ended up jammed together in the doorway.

We discovered later that the crash had been caused by a chim-

ney pot which had become dislodged and had fallen onto the cor-
rugated iron roof — right above my head.

13

The hazards of army life

There was an annual religious ceremony among the Gurkhas known as Dashera. It was a rather gruesome affair involving the beheading of various animals.

In phase one of the operation the senior Gurkha officer was to behead a small buffalo. This was done with a double-handed sacrificial *kukhri*. The animal had to be completely beheaded with one single blow. It was believed that failure to do this would bring bad luck to the regiment. This was carried out to the accompaniment of much applause from the assembled crowd.

As the last-joined officer to the brigade I was invited to take part in the Dashera ceremony, but I wasn't sure what my part was to be. A goat was produced and I was handed a *kukhri* and shown where to strike the fatal blow. Even though I was a veteran of World War I and had witnessed death in many forms, when that innocent goat looked up into my face I just couldn't bring myself to do it. I made some futile excuse, and I think the Gurkha understood how I felt. In any event, they presented me with two *kukhris* — one "dress" to be worn on special occasions with a blue velvet scabbard and silver trimmings and the other a normal regimental *kukhri*. I still treasure them today.

Like all good things, my time at Abbottabad eventually came to an end, and I was ordered to proceed to a new station called

Rawalpindi, the headquarters of Northern Command and Rawalpindi district.

I joined a battery in the 22nd Field Brigade Royal Artillery.
The following morning I was to report to the colonel. His name
was C.M.H. Stevens. He was to be responsible for changing my
whole future in the army, although I didn't realise it at the time.
I walked into the colonel's office accompanied by my C.O., a
grand chap by the name of Major Torquil-McLeod.

As I approached his desk he looked up and said: "Oh, Hodgson,
I see you've just come from a staff job. I hope you're not one of
these fellows always looking for these jobs? I think a spell of regimental duty will do you good. I notice that you've done the
Weedon course — we'll need you here as the standard of riding
is damn bad."

It wasn't a very encouraging reception, and from that day on
we always seemed to be at loggerheads.

I remember one day in particular, during an officers' riding
class. Riding instruction was in progress to some twenty officers
and the long whip was lying on the tan. My colonel had come into
the manège, unnoticed by me, and I was continuing with my
instructions. I turned and saw the colonel, who by this time had
picked up the long whip and was flicking the horses as they went
round. This rather annoyed me, and to register a silent protest I
joined the ride. Suddenly there was a shout! "Hodgson, what the
hell do you think you're doing?"

So I left the ride and rode up to the old boy, saluted and said:
"Sorry Sir, but I thought you'd taken over the ride."

"I don't like your attitude Hodgson," he said, "I hope you're
not being impertinent. I'll see you in my office later."

I think I was very unwise to behave as I did, but I felt that
I had some justification. The way he just barged in and appeared
to take over the ride without even greeting me, I felt, was tactless
in the extreme.

Later on in his office, the colonel repeated his previous remarks
and said that he had taken great exception to my behaviour, and
asked for an explanation. I told him that I was merely carrying out
what we had been taught at Weedon, where the use of the long

whip on such an occasion would have been regarded as rank heresy. I then apologised to the old boy, but I don't think my explanation satisfied him and from then on our relations were even more strained.

Despite this inauspicious start in Rawalpindi I quite enjoyed my time there. I formed a polo team and we played some good games against the Indian Cavalry. I also managed to get a show jumping team going among the N.C.O s which we entered for the Northern Command Horse Show. In a private capacity I used to teach the local army nursing sisters to ride. This was a lot more difficult than my army duties as they wouldn't do as they were told!

As a result of my deal with the Maharajah of Patiala I was in a position to buy several unbacked ponies, which I eventually sold at quite a good profit. I was fortunate in having a good Indian horse dealer from whom I bought a number of well-bred "green" ponies, for which I paid one thousand rupees and more. I then set about breaking them in and training them in my spare time. Here again, Suba Khan was invaluable as he had been trained at Sauger, the equivalent of Weedon in the Indian Army.

One day the colonel sent for me and with much foreboding I went along to his office. He told me that the Royal Horse, Royal Field and Royal Garrison Artillery were to be amalgamated into one regiment to be called the Royal Artillery. With a cynical smile on his face he said: "I have recommended you for the Garrison Artillery."

"Have I no choice, Sir?" I said. "I've always been a Field Gunner and wish to remain so. I would be a square peg in a round hole in the Garrison Artillery."

The colonel replied: "My recommendation stands."

I left his office feeling very angry as I knew his recommendation was merely out of spite. I was determined not to leave it there. Although the standard of gunnery in the Garrison was very high, the thought of being stuck in a fort for the rest of my army career didn't appeal to me at all. But as a mere lieutenant what on earth could I do?

Luckily I had a good friend in the Brigadier Royal Artillery of the district, a chap called Metcalfe with whom I'd served at the battle of Le Cateau in World War I and the same officer that I'd seen at the War Office before leaving for India. As I felt that my situation called for extreme measures I went to his office at Northern Command Headquarters.

After I had told the brigadier my tale of woe he pointed out that this was an extremely unorthodox way of doing things, but owing to our long friendship he was prepared to overlook it. He said that he was coming to see my colonel the following morning and that I would be sent for. Laughingly, he said: "Now — get out!"

Next morning in the colonel's office the B.R.A. said to me: "I presume that you understand about this proposed amalgamation of the regiment? I propose to recommend you for the Horse Artillery, with a second choice of Field Artillery."

The brigadier then turned to Colonel Stevens and said: "I'm sure that you agree with this, don't you, Stevens?"

Of course my colonel must have known that it was a put-up job, but he had no alternative but to agree. I left his office in a much happier frame of mind.

At my next meeting with the colonel he made it quite plain that he knew I had side-stepped him. I apologised, but said that in my own interests I had been forced to take drastic steps.

Despite injections for all known diseases which were common in India, we occasionally used to get the odd case of enteric amongst our military personnel. The wife of one of our chaps was just getting over a go of enteric in the Military Hospital. Her bed had been wheeled out into the garden, and the patient was asleep.

By mistake a nurse had placed some tea and toast at her bed-side. The patient was still not well enough to eat any solid food. Luckily, before the sick woman had woken up a kitehawk had swooped down and grabbed the toast from the plate, and thereby saved her life.

Shortly afterwards the nurse, realising her mistake, rushed into the garden and, seeing the empty plate, said to her patient in a frantic voice: "Oh my goodness, you haven't eaten that have you?"

102

Of course the woman didn't know what she was talking about as she had been asleep, but had she eaten the toast she would probably have died from perforation of the intestine.

Still on the subject of diseases, I was due to have my tonsils out, and prior to the operation I had to have certain tests. One of these was a swab test in my throat. The next afternoon I was playing polo, and on arriving back at the bungalow found a car in the compound. One of the doctors from the hospital was waiting for me.

"I'm afraid you'll have to come into hospital immediately," he said. "We've discovered that you are a typhoid carrier."

"Good heavens," I said. "What's the hurry and what does it involve?"

"Well," he said. "You'll be in the isolation ward for at least six weeks. No visitors allowed. Get changed and come with me at once.'

So I was put into bed in the rather grim isolation ward and shortly afterwards the doctor appeared and gave me a huge injection with a syringe about the size of a bicycle pump. He then told me that if I was ever taken ill I must tell the doctor I had had this special anti-typhoid injection, as you were only supposed to have it once in a lifetime.

The thought of six weeks in solitary confinement dispelled any thought of sleep that night. The fact that I felt perfectly well was even more frustrating. My clothes had been taken away so any hope of escape was out of the question.

Next morning the doctor appeared with a smile on his face: "Terribly sorry, old chap, we've bungled it. The swabs got mixed up and you're not a carrier after all. You can go as soon as you like."

There was a bit of a fuss about the whole thing and shortly afterwards the M.O. responsible was sent back to England.

Our lives in the British Army in India were divided into roughly two seasons, the hot weather and the cold. The hot season lasted from about March to September. That part of the year was uninteresting in every way. All the wives and families of both officers and N.C.O.s went up to the hills, and also all the British infantry regiments.

At this time of year we used to get up before dawn, while it was still reasonably cool, and were on parade by 6 a.m. Whatever training was necessary was carried out by 9 a.m. and the horses were fed, groomed and watered, by which time the day's outdoor training was over. After a late breakfast we would be back in the office by 10 a.m. to start our administrative work.

By noon the day's work was over and we would go off to the mess for a drink and lunch. After lunch we would go to our bungalows to "study for the staff college," which usually meant having a bit of shut-eye. By then it was too fiendishly hot to do anything else. After tea we would play squash, tennis, polo or golf, all of which were available at the club. Then it was time to change and go back to the mess for dinner.

It was really a pretty good life, apart from the heat and the lack of feminine company. The clubs were an important and integral part of our social lives; every cantonment had one, and all officers and their wives were eligible for membership.

At the beginning of June, just when you were beginning to feel suicidal from the heat, eaten alive with mosquitoes and covered with prickly heat, the monsoon broke. The temperature dropped considerably and it rained continuously for about three months, accompanied by thunder and lightning. This caused great devastation and flooding, the rivers overflowed their banks and millions of people were left homeless. After three months of rain and mud with fungus all over your shoes and clothes, you began to wonder if the heat wasn't preferable to the monsoon.

By September, conditions had improved considerably. The rains had stopped and the weather was cooler. The wives started to come back from the hills and our social life was resumed. However, this was constantly interrupted by long periods of training and manoeuvres, which had to be carried out during the cold weather. So life in India for a married officer was one of constant separation. In fact I used to carry a photograph of my wife so that when I got back from these long periods of absence I wouldn't go to the wrong wife! These separations naturally led to a lot of marital trouble and infidelity, especially as there were about

Lt. C.F. Hodgson in 1918. The armband denotes that he has been a war hospital patient and his sleeve badges that he has given three years' service in France.

Lt. Hodgson and his Irish bride, Florence McConnell, on their wedding day in February, 1918 (Page 42).

*The photographs on this page show some of
the conditions of warfare in France and
Belgium during World War I. Above:
British troops strain to move a gun into
position. Below: British troops in a
trench. (Chapters 1 to 5)*

Above: A coach and four used by officers at Norwich for their transport (Pages 53-55). Right: The author's wife, Florence, and "Mr. Wubbins", the puppy which travelled across India on ice. (page 114). Below: Bound for India. The S.S. Syria sails from Tilbury Docks with the author and his wife on board (Page 67).

Left: A typical Indian bearer. Note the Gunner colours on his turban. Below: The boat used for crocodile shooting. This one was holed by the author in his struggle with a wounded crocodile. (Page 112). Right: An Afridi tribesman waiting to snipe at some unsuspecting Britisher. (Page 152).

Left: The author and his wife in 1942, when he was O.C. Chaklala in the Punjab (Page 183). Right top: A typical officer's bungalow in the Punjab. Ferozepore, 1927 (Page 110). Right: "Tum-Tum Tommy", a pony, pulling a governess-cart. This was the same pony, harnessed to a cart, which had to swim a river in spate (Page 76). Below: Grey Dawn, the polo pony which the author sold to the Maharajah of Patiala (Page 85).

Left: Pack ponies on trek in Chamba (Page 131). Below: The red bear shot in Chamba in the Himalayas. Kumla, the shikari, is on the right (Page 137).

Above: "The Field Kitchen" at rest. The author sits on the running board with his Gurkha orderly in attendance. (Page 131).
Below: The Balambhat bridge on the Swat river after the Mohmands had blown it up and (inset) the Bailey bridge which was built by Sappers as a temporary replacement (Page 154).

Above: The author shows Field Marshal, Sir Claude Auchinleck, a model of the new ordnance depot at Quetta in 1946. (Page 193). Left: A typical rope bridge on the way to Chamba (Page 132).

*Above: Colonel Hodgson, as secretary of the Durban branch of the 1820
Settlers Association, with a group of young settlers (Page 199).
Below: The author and his wife at Hilton, Natal, after he had retired from
the secretaryship of the 1820 Settlers Association.*

Right: The author in 1927, then a major, wearing the full dress uniform of the Royal Artillery. Below: The majestic Himalayas.

ten men to every woman among the white officers.

The coming of cooler weather was the signal for the "fishing fleet" to set sail from England. This consisted of large numbers of young women, daughters and relations of officers who used to come out each year in search of husbands.

Some of these girls really fancied themselves. On one occasion my wife and I gave a dinner party prior to a dance which was being held at the club. We had invited about half a dozen of these young anglers as partners for our junior officers.

In those days we all had programmes for dances which were booked in advance. Each dance was numbered and there were a certain number of "extras" which followed on. As host I felt I should ask one of the girls for a dance. She looked at her programme and said: "You can have the tenth "extra".

I politely told her what to do with her "tenth extra." As her host it would have been more polite to have offered me one of the early "chukkas." It wasn't considered the thing to book dances before the dinner party, but the girls were so much in demand that they lost all sense of proportion.

When on manoeuvres we used to move up and down the Grand Trunk Road. At that time this was the main road between Calcutta and Peshawar. All along the road one would see the bodies of cattle that had died from disease or exhaustion. The carcasses would be covered with hundreds of vultures who picked the bones bare, thus performing a very necessary hygienic service. Within seconds of an animal falling, they would be on the body.

Sad, but interesting features of the Grand Trunk Road were the many cemeteries which were found next to the camps that were dotted along this road. We used these camps during manoeuvres.

These cemeteries were relics of the very early days of the British occupation of India. They contained the remains of all ranks of the British Army and their families who had died during the last century — mainly of cholera and malaria — at a very early age. One frequently read inscriptions on the tombstones such as:

"Mrs Angela Smith, wife of Sgt Smith, died of cholera aged 18 15th February, 1860."

Some of the unfortunate deceased were as young as fifteen.

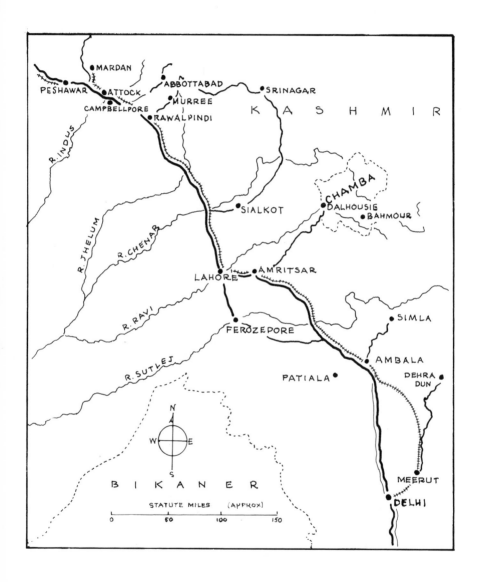

During my time in India the social life of the British soldier was always a problem. There were no white women and no pubs. Any girl-friends he had were usually among the Anglo-Indian or Coloured girls, as the Indian women were usually in *purdah* and in any case didn't associate with Europeans.

When I first arrived most of the units in the cantonments had what could be described as brothels. These were under strict medical supervision and consequently the incidence of venereal disease was very low.

Then a new Viceroy was appointed. The Vicereign was a bit of a do-gooder, and she was absolutely horrified to learn that the British units had what were tantamount to brothels in their lines. Orders were received that these places were to be closed immediately. We protested, pointing out that if they were closed the incidence of V.D. would rise very sharply, much to the detriment of the efficiency of the army. After all, the British Tommy couldn't be expected to live like a monk during the years that he was in India.

Anyway, the authorities took no notice and the soldiers' source of comfort was cut off. And, of course, as we had predicted, V.D. rocketed, but they wouldn't rescind the order.

While I was in Rawalpindi I had to deal with the case of a young soldier who had contracted V.D. He had to go into hospital and when he came out he was brought up on a charge. As his C.O. I had to deduct a day's pay for every day he'd been in hospital, as it was considered to be a self-inflicted illness. As he had been in hospital for a month it was quite a big deduction.

I had a long talk to this young fellow and asked him how it had happened.

"Well, Sir," he said, "you know there's not much to do here, and there are not many girls of our class. We're more or less forced to associate with the coloured girls. I went for a walk rather late one night and walked up the Mall in 'Pindi. I was accosted by a *tonga wallah* (the chap who drives a *tonga* or single horse type of trap.) He made certain suggestions to me and I agreed, so we drove out to Topi Park. There he produced an Indian woman who agreed to my proposition and that was that. The *tonga wallah* then collected his fee and drove me back to barracks. I carried out the usual prophylactic precautions and forgot all about it. Then, some time later, to my horror, I found I had V.D."

I told him that I felt we ought to do something about this woman as she would be handing the horrible disease on to other fellows.

"Come on," I said to him, "we'll do a practice run tonight." So we went out together and he met the same *tonga wallah,* who came up with the same suggestion, and out we drove to Topi Park. I was dressed in mufti so the *tonga wallah* didn't know who I was.

Sure enough when we got to the appointed place a woman emerged from behind the bushes. It was very dark and I shone my torch on her. A more loathsome, filthy, diseased-looking old hag I have yet to see. I said to the young fellow: "What on earth did you go with a thing like that for, don't you feel revolted?"

"Well," he said, "it was dark so I couldn't see what she looked like and I'd had a few drinks — you know what it's like, Sir. I've definitely learnt my lesson, it won't happen again."

We put the woman in the *tonga* and drove back to the cantonment where we handed her over to the police. I felt we had taught that young fellow a lesson. He was such a nice clean, fair-haired young Englishmen, aged about nineteen, but possibly ruined for life through a moment of thoughtlessness.

14

Goodbye to the regiment

Although I was happy enough in my unit and with life generally in 'Pindi, promotion in the regiment was painfully slow. Promotion came about only by vacancy, so it was a case of "dead men's shoes," and already I had been a subaltern for over ten years.

One night in the club I met a brigadier, ex-Royal Artillery, who had transferred to the Indian Army. We were discussing my prospects, or lack of them, and he said: "Your obvious line of action is to transfer to the Indian Army. It would mean faster promotion, better pay and better prospects. I did it and I've never regretted it."

I discussed it with my major who thought it was a good idea, so I prepared an application which he signed. The prospect of leaving the regiment saddened me considerably, but it was a question of "needs must when the devil drives." But it wasn't going to be as easy as I thought. Within a few days of signing my application for transfer the colonel sent for me. He said: "About this application of yours – I'm not going to sign it."

I asked him the reason for this and he wouldn't give me a satisfactory reply. Of course, without my colonel's signature on it I thought my application would not be acceptable, so I withdrew feeling very unhappy about the situation. I felt he was just being bloody-minded.

I then went to see my friend, Brigadier Finnies, and told him my position. To my surprise he said: "Oh! That's all right, I'll arrange it."

Some three weeks later, to my great surprise, I received a letter from army headquarters to say that my application to the Indian Army (Indian Army Ordnance Corps) had been accepted on a two-year probation period. I was to proceed at the earliest opportunity and report to the chief ordnance officer at the Arsenal in Ferozepore.

My colonel then sent for me again and for some reason didn't query how I'd managed to get the transfer accepted. He just said: "I hope you realise that there's no question of your coming back to the regiment once you leave."

Then his whole attitude seemed to change. He said: "Hodgson, I appear to have misjudged you, and I have a proposition to make. Withdraw your application to transfer and I will appoint you as my adjutant, which will bring an increase in pay. Also I will recommend you for accelerated promotion."

"It's very kind of you, Sir," I replied, "but I've made up my mind and I'm going to proceed with the transfer."

Subsequently the regiment gave me a terrific send-off in the mess, at which the colonel presided. To hear him speak of my achievements you would have thought I was his "blue-eyed boy." In due course, the regimental cup containing champagne was passed round and came to me first as the guest of honour. I then handed it to the colonel and in doing so "inadvertently" tilted the cup which upset some of the champagne down his shirt front. However, he was so full of goodwill by this time that even that didn't upset him — or perhaps it was relief at my departure!

So it was that in September of 1927 I sold all my beloved polo ponies except Larry, my charger, and we packed up and moved to Ferozepore with much foreboding. It was a completely new life and foreign to anything that I'd previously undertaken.

Ferozepore was a small cantonment, rather similar to Campbellpore. It was situated some thirty miles from Lahore, the capital of the Punjab, on the left bank of the Sutlej river. The countryside was as flat as a pancake and the climate was stinking hot in summer and reasonably good in winter.

One of the conditions of final acceptance into the Indian Army was that I passed an exam in Urdu, both oral and written, within the probationary period. I optimistically thought that I'd acquired sufficient knowledge to pass without further tuition, and confidently sat for the exam at the first opportunity. However, when I took the exam I realised that my chances of passing were pretty slim, and this was confirmed when I received the results. I had failed miserably and the examiner's comment was: "If you've got *a munchi* (teacher) sack him; if you haven't — get one!"

I realised that I'd jumped the gun and that I'd have to get down to some serious study. Fortunately I passed at the second attempt and the benign government graciously gave me a reward of one hundred and fifty rupees for my trouble. This was really to help defray the expense of employing a *munchi*.

Accommodation at Ferozepore was difficult for married officers, and we had to live in a *dak* bungalow for a couple of weeks.

We were then fortunate enough to meet the Sessions Judge, a man called Abraham. He invited us to take over his very nice bungalow and run it for him. As his wife spent most of her time in the U.K. he really wanted a hostess to entertain his guests. This my wife was only too pleased to do in return for living in such comfortable surroundings. The judge was a charming and interesting man. Born in the Channel Islands, he spoke French fluently and had acted as interpreter to Georges Clemenceau at the Treaty of Versailles Conference.

One of the people we entertained at his bungalow was a Major Attlee, later to become Prime Minister of England. He was heading the Geddes Commission at the time, which was investigating conditions in India with a view to giving it self-government. I found him a very approachable man and we used to talk for hours.

Judge Abraham was quite a wit in a dry sort of way. I remember a dance one evening at which he was host. Some fussy old dame came up to him and said: "So nice to meet you, Mr. Abrahams."

To which he replied: "How do you do Madame? My name is in

the singular, my decorations in the plural."

As the judge used to deal with all the murder cases, I asked him one day how on earth he could tell who was speaking the truth, as many Indians were such inveterate liars. He told me one infallible method was to watch their feet rather than their faces. If they were lying they invariably wiggled their big toes.

The judge had to be present at the frequent hangings and often asked me to go with him. I simply couldn't face it, especially as they were usually before breakfast.

One of the chief forms of sport was shooting *mugger* or crocodile. The particular species found at Ferozepore, on the river Sutlej, were called *ghariyal,* a fish-eating crocodile with a very long slender muzzle and rows of vicious-looking teeth.

My first effort at getting a croc was rather a farce, as I completely underestimated the range across the water and found I had shot a croc of about four feet long. It looked more like a large lizard. We had him stuffed and kept him as a trophy. On this particular trip I was accompanied by my wife and a young brother officer. We got to the river by means of a buckboard and then transferred ourselves and our equipment into a flat-bottomed boat. This was about twenty-four feet long by ten feet wide and had a crew of three, plus a *shikari.* It was propelled by rowing and also had a sail. After shooting the "lizard" we continued downstream with no effort needed on the part of the crew as the river was running swiftly.

On either side of the river were numerous sandbanks on which crocs of all sizes were sunbathing. There were also hundreds of fresh-water turtles — some of them enormous things about four feet long.

Presently the *shikari* shouted out: *Mugger — mugger much.* (Hindustani in the vernacular for a fish-eating croc, *much* meaning fish.)

We looked through our binoculars and this time we could see that it was indeed a huge chap. The next operation was to beach the boat as it wasn't feasible to shoot the croc from the boat. The shikari and I took up our positions on the bank and I fired two shots, one into his neck and the other into his tail, and he appeared to be dead. Once back in the boat we went off to retrieve our trophy, which in this instance was lying on a sandbank in mid-stream. We came alongside and the crew lifted him into the boat. He was a colossal fellow, about twelve feet long. The *shikari* tied him up to the rowlock with a piece of rope round his jaws. Off we went down the river in pursuit of a trophy for my friend Donald Way.

Suddenly there was pandemonium in the little boat. Our "dead" croc had come to life, had broken loose from his rope and was flaying his tail about and snapping at everyone with his lethal jaws.

Of course everyone was panic stricken, and I realised that some-thing had to be done, and quickly. So I opened up on him with my rifle, fired several shots and put paid to his antics. Unfortun-ately in the excitement a couple of the bullets had gone through the bottom of the boat. Water started pouring in and the boat started to sink. To make matters worse we were right in mid-stream, and the Sutlej river at this point was about two hundred yards wide and full of crocs. My wife started to panic, and we frantically rowed for the shore — making it just in time. A couple of times I thought that the crew was going to bale out.

We beached the boat and the croc, and I gave it a couple more shots, just to make sure. The members of the crew then had to set about making the boat seaworthy, which they managed to do quite quickly and we continued our voyage down river.

Back we went to Ferozepore where we dined out on our croc shoot for some time to come. We sent the skins to a tannery at Cawnpore where they were made into suitcases, shoes, handbags and a couple of blotters, some of which I have to this day.

Some of the chaps in the cantonment used to make quite a little income on the side by croc-shooting and selling the tanned skins in England. Even in those days they fetched a good price.

My C.O. in Ferozepore was an ex-gunner called Colonel Finnies, brother of the Brigadier who had persuaded me to join the Indian Army. He was a most friendly, helpful sort of chap. One morning he said to me: "I'm sending you down to Kirkee near Poona for a year's course in ordnance work, and if you pass you will get a qualification after your name. I want you to do very well on the course and get a 'distinguished.' Your predecessor did, and I expect you to do the same, or better. If you do well there will be a good job for you as an inspecting ordnance officer. You'll find this interesting, but you will need to have a car."

At this time we had a very special terrier, known to her friends as Pegs. Despite all precautions she managed to produce endless litters of pups, all of very doubtful parenthood on the paternal side. About a week before we left for Kirkee, Pegs produced a litter of six pups. It was obvious that we couldn't keep them all as we were soon leaving, so we disposed of five of them. The next day when I looked into her basket I found that there were three little fellows there instead of one. On closer inspection I found that the other two were in fact kittens belonging to a wild cat that Pegs had discovered in the garden. So I then had to set about finding the wild cat's lair and replacing the kittens.

Pegs repeated this operation several times until the wild cat and her litter changed their abode.

As the journey to Kirkee was going to take three days by train and would be extremely hot, we had to devise a plan to get the puppy there safely. We took huge blocks of ice wrapped in sacking, which we put in our private lavatory where the dog basket was kept. So it was that Pegs and her son, whom we christened Mr. Wubbins, travelled to Kirkee on ice. The little pup grew up into a delightful companion and lived with us for the next thirteen years.

Kirkee was situated some 60 miles from Bombay in the Ghats. These were a range of hills running down the centre of India. The climate was pleasantly cool, and remained the same the whole year round. Tiger were quite numerous in this part of India, which had lush vegetation providing them with cover. I went out on several tiger shoots, but never saw one, although one could often hear them calling. Bird life was prolific, and even near our bungalow we had masses of hoopoes, bulbuls, fiscal shrikes, mynahs, hawks and jungle fowl.

Bearing in mind the Colonel's instructions I worked very diligently and managed, at the end of the year's course, to get a "distinguished" with honours.

15

A learner driver and his first car

When the course ended I realised that I would have to buy a car in order to do the job that I'd been promised. So at the age of thirty-one I acquired my first car, a Fiat, twelve horse power.

At this stage I couldn't drive. My wife, who had driven some years before in Ireland, made the fatal mistake of volunteering to teach me. We had many altercations, and I'm sure I wasn't an easy pupil. On one memorable occasion my wife was giving me a lesson in the middle of the Maidan, a big open space where we did our training. She became so exasperated that she simply got out of the car and said quietly: "I can't take any more — get yourself home." And off she went, leaving her terrified husband alone with a strange car in the middle of India.

This treatment of being "thrown in the deep end" was really the best thing that could have happened, of course. I just had to get myself home, a distance of some two miles. I managed to get the car into second gear and eventually ground and crawled back home, feeling rather pleased with myself.

I managed to pass my test and became a licensed driver, but the real test was to come some few weeks later when we had to take our car, dogs, ourselves and all our possessions back to Ferozepore, a journey of some thirteen hundred miles over dirt roads which were very dusty. I felt this was no mean feat for a driver of a few weeks standing.

Within a few hours of starting we nearly came to grief. Passing through a village we came upon a herd of domestic buffalo, some of them with calves. I was edging my way through them when suddenly one of the cows with a calf charged the car. By a bit of manipulation I just managed to avoid the full impact of the six-foot spread of horns, and we suffered nothing worse than a dent all along one side of my new car. The buffalo's horns were so vicious that they could easily have gone right through the body-work.

The next natural hazard that we had to contend with was the crossing of the Godavari river. When we got to the bank we found the river in full spate and that the only means of crossing was by a flat-bottomed boat manned by several Indians. I got out of the car and did a "recce" to find out the modus operandi. As the river was in flood the boat was riding exceptionally high, and in order to get the car on board you had to drive it up on two planks laid at an angle of about 45 degrees. From this acute angle all you could see was the sky.

Further encouragement came from the boatman, who said that the previous day a man had driven up on to the deck, failed to stop, and had gone into the river on the other side.

"Look, there's his car still in the water," said the boatman enthusiastically pointing into the river.

I felt that I was completely incapable of dealing with this problem, and in fact was in a blue funk. I tried my best to get out of doing the job, and suggested to one of the boat crew that they might drive the car on board. They all declined with thanks. I then turned to my wife and said that as my instructor and an experienced driver I felt sure that she would be able to handle this situation. However, she said that nothing would induce her to try it.

We waited by the river for some time in the hope that another vehicle would come along, so that we could make use of the driver, but nobody came. We then decided that as we couldn't spend the rest of my army service on the banks of the Godavari river, there was no alternative but to make the attempt.

I told my wife to get out and take the dogs with her as there was no point in us both getting drowned. We removed as much of the luggage as we could. Then, sweating profusely, with my pulse racing, I put the car into bottom gear and with the hand-brake on I started up those hideously narrow planks — inch by inch. I could see absolutely nothing but the sky above, so there was nothing by which I could steer. By the grace of God and little apples I got to the top. The crewman handled the car and got it down onto the deck. The driver tottered out and collapsed into a jelly-like mass beside it!

My wife then "walked the plank" carrying the dogs; the luggage was brought on board and the crossing began. The boat was really a pont, which was propelled across the river by means of a rope pulled by several Indians. Once across the river getting the car off the boat was a much less hazardous business. We still had to contend with the planks, but you could see where you were going and there was terra firma ahead.

We spent the first night at Aurungabad, a very interesting Hindu town containing some historic temples, some of which we visited.

Four days and seven punctures later we arrived in Agra, where we intended to spend several days sight-seeing. The punctures were mainly due to picking up loose bullock shoes, with which all the roads in India were liberally sprinkled.

Of course the main attraction of Agra was the Taj Mahal. We had planned our journey so as to be in Agra at full moon, so that we could admire the magnificent marble mausoleum in its full glory. And what a breath-taking sight it was. No wonder it is one of the seven wonders of the world. It was built by Shah Jehan in memory of his beloved wife Mumtaz Mahal, who died in 1631 while giving birth to her fifteenth child. Started in 1632, it took thirty years to complete and cost forty million rupees, or about half-a-million pounds.

He brought masons from Italy to work on the white marble screen in the burial chamber. This screen was made of one huge piece of marble, intricately carved and inlaid with precious stones in a floral design. Once the work in the burial chamber was completed it is said that Shah Jehan had the Italian craftsmen blinded so that the work could never be repeated. Altogether some twenty thousand workmen were employed in building the Taj. We were told that during the Indian Mutiny the British Tommies looted many of the precious stones by digging them out with their bayonets. The stones were subsequently replaced with semi-precious ones.

Not satisfied with this one memorial to his wife, Shah Jehan set about building various other monuments and buildings. He built eleven thrones, the most famous of them being the Peacock Throne, which is now in Iran.

While in Agra we visited Fatehpur Sikri and saw one of these thrones. It was in the shape of a peacock, its tail, which formed the back of the throne, being picked out in precious stones. The peacock's back formed the seat of the throne, with the highly decorated crested head protruding forward.

We were told by our guide that on completion of these various buildings Shah Jehan's son Aurangzeb, worried by his father's great extravagance and thinking that there would be nothing left for him, had his father murdered. However, I have since read that in fact he had him imprisoned in the fort at Agra, where he died in 1666, so there is probably some truth in both accounts. Aurangzeb, after a family feud with his three brothers, declared himself emperor in 1658.

Having seen the sights of Agra and recovered from our long journey, we set out for Delhi.

About twenty miles short of Delhi we were tootling along the road, sending up clouds of the interminable dust, when I noticed two women in *bourkhas* standing on the right-hand side of the road. They were carrying *tolas* (small brass containers) and *chattis* (earthenware containers) on their heads. I slowed down and hooted and then, to my horror, just as I got abreast of them one of the women started to run across the road in front of me. I imagine she was trying to avoid the dust. I braked and swerved, but as I was doing about forty at the time there was no way that I could avoid her. I took her up by the roots, she went right over the bonnet, onto the roof and slid down the back.

Of course the *chatti* came unstuck and so did the *tola*. The earthenware *chatti* hit the upright support of the windscreen and broke into several pieces, some of which hit my wife in the face. As the windscreen was of the type that could be opened at the top, the pieces of *chatti* luckily went clean through without shattering the glass. The *tola,* which contained curry, deposited its contents on the roof, which then oozed and dripped down the sides of the car.

By the time I had brought the car to a halt my wife's face was bleeding profusely, but she insisted that she was all right and that I must go and look at the Indian woman.

I walked back and found the woman lying in the middle of the road. She looked just like a motionless bundle of white cloth. I spoke to her in Hindustani and got no response, so I bent down and touched her and there was no sign of life. I didn't dare remove her *bourkha* as this would have caused more trouble, and there didn't seem to be anyone around. The woman who had been with her seemed to have vanished. I was just wondering what on earth to do next when I heard a noise of stamping feet behind me. I turned round, and there, to my great relief, standing to attention and saluting was a smartly dressed Indian who announced: "I am ex-Subadar Major Ranjit Singh," and he mentioned some Indian regiment.

"I'm very pleased that you're here, Subadar Sahib," I said. "What on earth am I going to do about this woman?"

He smilingly replied: *Kuch ficker nain, Sahib, yej surif aurat hai.* (Don't worry, it's only a woman.)

I said I was worried that she might be dead, to which he again replied that it didn't matter as she was only a woman. I said that it was all very well, but we must do something for her.

The Subadar still said there was nothing to worry about and I must go on with my journey and leave it to him.

So I gave him my name and address in Ferozepore along with fifty rupees. I took his name and address as well, and left him with instructions to get the poor woman to the nearest hospital or somewhere where she could get medical attention. Should she become worse or die he was to communicate with me.

Acha Sahib, the Subadar said and saluted. Then he went up

to this bundle of cloth, spoke to her in her own dialect, kicked her, and the wretched creature, still completely enveloped in her *bourkha,* crawled to the side of the road. I felt dreadful about the whole thing, but didn't know what else I could do, and as my wife was in need of urgent medical attention herself I decided that we must press on to Delhi, about fifteen miles away.

As we approached the Delhi cantonment I stopped at the first police station that we came to and went in to report the accident. There were two sub-inspectors, Anglo-Indians, sitting at a table. I spoke to them in English and one said to the other in Hindustani. "What does this fool want to come here and report an accident for? He should have done it further back — the idiot."

I then spoke to them in Hindustani and gave them a rocket for their rudeness. In a flash I had them on their feet saluting with both hands!

We carried on to the hospital at Delhi where my wife received treatment for her cuts and an anti-tetanus injection. We spent a couple of days resting in Delhi, and my wife was none the worse apart from having the most enormous black eye I have ever seen. The bruise stretched from her left temple right down to her neck. When we got back to Ferozepore there was a good deal of leg pulling about my wife's appearance and despite my explanation I became known as the Wife Beater!

The C.O. was very pleased with my efforts at Kirkee and as promised he appointed me inspecting ordnance officer for an area approximately one thousand miles long by five hundred broad. The job involved inspecting and testing explosives held by all units in that area, including artillery, cavalry, infantry, engineers and the native states. All the maharajahs and rajahs in those days had their own armies, and among the ones that fell under my jurisdiction were the Maharajahs of Patiala, Bikaner and Gwalior and the Nawab of Mamdot.

It was an extremely interesting job and involved a tremendous amount of travelling, an average of two to three thousand miles a month. So the newly-fledged driver had a lot of practice in his little twelve horse Fiat.

Mamdot was a tiny state near Ferozepore. Its ruler, the Nawab, was by far the biggest man I have ever seen. Some idea of his size will be given by the fact that we used one of his polo boots in the mess as an umbrella stand, a job usually done by an elephant's foot! The Nawab used to play polo or, rather, come onto the field on his pony. He would then sit in the middle of the field and should the ball come in his direction he would have a swipe at it. Even the biggest polo pony couldn't possibly gallop with him on board, so any fast movement was out of the question. Like many large people he had a jovial and likeable personality and was very popular with the British officers.

The state of Bikaner was a vast area, and mostly desert. It had once been fertile ground, and the Maharajah was a well-educated and far-seeing man who had great ambition for his state. When the hydro-electric scheme was being built near Ferozepore the Maharajah had a very long concrete-lined canal built in order to channel water down to Bikaner and bring about a huge irrigation scheme.

In this way he hoped to restore the country to its former fertile state. The canal was about fifty miles long and cost the Maharajah something in the region of five million pounds.

On several occasions when I visited Bikaner on inspection work a sand grouse shoot was organised. These birds were very numerous in this semi-desert country when they used to come in huge flocks in the evening to their drinking places.

During his tour of India the Prince of Wales visited Bikaner and a sand grouse shoot was organised in his honour. H.R.H. couldn't understand why the birds took no notice of the guns, but came in to drink regardless of the noise and firing. He then discovered that the birds had been kept off the water for some days prior to his shoot so that the poor little devils were practically dying of thirst. On finding out about this the Prince refused to take any further part in the slaughter.

The Maharajah of Bikaner lived in the most sumptuous palace and was very hospitable. On my visits I was put up in a very comfortable guest house adjacent to the palace. My meals were served in the guest house and I was entertained by one of the A.D.Cs. I never met any of the womenfolk, who lived apart in the traditional Indian style, but was shown over the palace and met the Maharajah on several occasions. The first time he was reading a paper, so that his face was hidden, and when he spoke one could have mistaken his voice for that of an Englishman.

The Maharajah of Patiala was a great cricketer as well as being a keen sportsman and polo player. He specialised in lavish entertainment on a grand scale and went to great lengths to see that his guests were provided with every comfort. On one occasion some of our chaps went down to Patiala to play cricket. After a slap-up dinner, with wine flowing, entertainment was provided by Indian *nautch* girls. These were professional dancers who performed traditional Indian dances. One of our young cricketers, on going to his room at the end of the evening, found a beautiful white girl in his bed. Thinking he had got into the wrong room he went out again to check it. He then realised that this was the Maharajah's way of seeing that his guests were entertained at night as well as by day! According to our young cricketer he told the girl to get out, but I can't vouch for the accuracy of this statement! No-one believed me either when I told them about my experience at Dranoutre in Belgium!

The state of Gwalior was really out of my province, but I found it convenient to do my inspection en route to Bombay when I was going on leave. On one occasion when I was in Gwalior the old Maharajah was very anxious that I should go on a tiger shoot with him. He was going to organise the whole thing with elephants and the lot. However, as I was catching a boat in a couple of days' time I wasn't able to take advantage of his marvellous offer.

He showed me the entrance to a tunnel, which was by then blocked up. The Maharajah told me that this tunnel stretched from Gwalior to Agra, a distance of some fifty miles. He said that this had been built during an early period of Indian history, when persecution was rife, to enable people to escape from Agra. If the story was true, which I had no reason to doubt, it was an incredible feat of engineering.

16

1929 — Leave to England

All the private armies that I visited in these native states were well disciplined and of a high standard. Their uniforms, equipment, weapons and ammunition were supplied by the Indian Government on payment by the Indian princes.

One of the Indian Army stations that I had to inspect was a place called Dehra Dun, some three thousand feet up in the foothills of the Himalayas. From there one had a good view of Nanda Devi, which at some 25 600 feet is one of the world's highest mountains. Like many of the mountains in the Himalayas it was called after a Hindu god.

While inspecting one of the Gurkha units at Dehra Dun they complained about the malfunctioning of some of their hand grenades. I decided to carry out a firing test *in situ*. Having collected a number of samples my warrant officer and I proceeded to an isolated *nullah* or dried-up river bed. After my course at Kirkee I was supposed to be a ballistics expert.

Well, we threw some of these grenades and they all seemed to explode satisfactorily. Then I threw one which failed to explode. Fortunately I had noted where it fell. We waited some time just to see if it would function, but nothing happened so finally I said to my W.O.: "I think we'll have to go and examine that one and see what's wrong with it."

My warrant officer said, "All right Sir, I'll pop down and have a look at it."

"I threw the damn thing," I replied, "so I'll go and locate it. I think I know its exact position. You watch out from here while I go down and see if I can find it and you can bring back the body."

I walked down into this valley towards the grass where the grenade had fallen. I had a sort of premonition that it might still explode, so as I neared the spot I started to crawl on my hands and knees — and it was just as well I did. As I got to within about ten yards of the spot where I thought the grenade was lying I heard of sort of "click." So I lay flat on my face and sure enough the grenade exploded. Some pieces of metal whizzed over my head and, on examining my topee, I found that several bits had gone clean through it. Of course my W.O. came rushing down half expecting to find me dead, I think. I must say it was a pretty near thing, but once again for some unknown reason the gods had been on my side. In future tests I used more open ground and took greater precautions.

This visit to Dehra Dun seemed to be fraught with danger. The following day I went out fishing for *mahseer* on the river Aran. The *mahseer* is an enormous fish, some even growing to the size of a man. From a sporting angle they don't rank very high as they don't put up much of a fight. However, they are good eating despite being full of bones.

I was standing up to my waist in the river fishing with a spoon as bait when suddenly I heard a grunting noise. Looking up I saw a troop of *langoor* monkeys sitting on the opposite bank. The *langoor* is a biggish animal, with a black face fringed with white hair. They have baboon-like bottoms.

The leader of the troop was a huge brute, about five feet high when he stood up. He was making a terrific noise and appeared to be urging the rest of the troop to attack me. I cogitated as to what action to take and wondered whether a monkey could swim. The *langoors* kept coming down to the water's edge and making horrible menacing noises, so I slowly retreated out of the water and on to the river bank where I had left my rifle. As I reached it the monkeys, lead by the enormous male, started to swim across the river, with the obvious intention of attacking. I grabbed my rifle and managed to shoot the leader just before he got to my side, and his body was swept away down stream.

I fired a few shots over the heads of the rest of the troop who then turned tail and swam back to the opposite side of the river and disappeared.

When I got back to mess in Dehra Dun where I was staying, I told them about my experience and they said I was lucky not to have been torn to pieces. Apparently these *langoor* monkeys are notoriously aggressive and savage, particularly when in large numbers, and will attack out of sheer devilment.

While in Dehra Dun I met a tea planter who was very anxious to find a good hack on which to ride around his tea estate. It occurred to me that my charger Larry would fit the bill, as unfortunately he was permanently disabled from a spavin. When I went on my course to Kirkee the question arose of finding a home for Larry during my absence. I decided to lend him to a young aspiring polo player in the Scots Fusiliers. I lent him on one condition — that the officer should insure him against all accidents and disease. This he promised faithfully to do.

While I was away Larry developed spavin trouble, a condition of the hock caused by ossification of the bones and consequent pain and lameness. When I got back from Kirkee, Larry's temporary owner came round in great distress to tell me about his condition. I told him that I naturally wouldn't hold him responsible as any horse could develop this condition, and in any case he was covered by insurance. The officer then confessed that he had not in fact done as promised and had Larry insured. I was rather angry about this, but he did offer to buy the horse.

I refused his offer, took Larry back and got in touch with the vet. The vet had some new theory for treating this condition, as opposed to "firing" which was not always successful. His treatment was to sever the affected tendon, thereby eliminating the pain which caused the horse to go lame. He thought that Larry would then be one hundred per cent. However, although the pain was apparently cured and he could walk without limping, he was no good as a polo pony, as he wasn't able to come back on his hocks and turn properly.

As I had no need of a charger in my new job, and I was shortly going on leave to the U.K., I felt that I couldn't find a better home for Larry than that promised by the planter in Dehra Dun. So my old friend was sent by rail to his new home where he settled down quite happily and where the soft terrain of the tea estate was suitable to his condition.

In 1929, having spent seven years in India and covered thirty five thousand miles in my little Fiat, we felt that it was about time to go on leave to the U.K.

On making application to be granted leave to England I was informed that I had forfeited my right to a passage at government expense as I was on probation to the Indian Army. For some reason which I could not fathom my wife would be granted a free passage in a troopship. I thought this was a highly unsatisfactory arrangement, but as I couldn't afford to pay for two return passages we decided to accept, especially as we hadn't seen our families for so long. I got the cheapest passage available for fifty pounds, sharing with three other army bods in an Anchor Line ship called the Tuscania.

Another snag was that we were sailing from different ports — my wife from Karachi and I from Bombay, a few days earlier. I was very distressed at leaving my wife in Ferozepore, and I think she was even more distressed at leaving our precious dogs behind!

I left Ferozepore and called in at Gwalior to do an inspection en route, which saved me over half my rail fare.

I arrived in Bombay the day before the ship sailed and booked in at a rather sleazy hotel. The bedrooms were sort of cubicles with no ceilings and little ventilation. I met a young subaltern at the hotel and we decided to spend as little time as possible there. We went out for dinner and then decided to have a look at the notorious Grant Road, Bombay's red light district.

We took a taxi and slowly drove down Grant Road. It was an amazing sight. Sitting behind barred windows were hundreds of prostitutes of many nationalities and in various states of undress. Most of the girls were white, but none of them was English, as they were banned from this lucrative profession. The taxi *wallah* took us to what he described as a "high class house," where we were met by the "Madame" and shown into the lounge.

We sat down and champagne was produced. Then the "girls," wearing only stockings and tiny panties, were paraded one at a time. We had no intention of taking advantage of the facilities offered, but we were just interested to see what these places were like. Two of the girls sat down and had a drink with us — they were French and very attractive — and they seemed to be reasonably happy with their situation.

After a time we asked for our bill. The "Madame" was most upset that we weren't going to take any further part in the proceedings. I think she felt that it was a reflection on her girls. Anyway, she charged us the full rate for the facilities which had been offered although not accepted. Only fair in the circumstances, I suppose. Anyway, it gave us an insight into the lives of these unfortunate women.

The taxi *wallah,* having apparently gleaned that things hadn't turned out according to plan, offered to take us to an even smarter "joint" in Colaba outside the red light district. However, by this time we'd had enough of the seamy side of Bombay and went back to our sumptuous hotel.

The next morning we embarked on the S.S. Tuscania and I met my three stable companions. One of them was a captain in the Indian Army and the other two were young second lieutenants in the Gunners. We managed to persuade the two young Gunners that as the voyage was likely to be hot they would be much more comfortable sleeping on the deck. They were happy to do this so cabin-wise we were quite comfortable.

The voyage proceeded pleasantly enough and we all had a good time. When we got into the Mediterranean it was decided to hold a farewell concert. I was appointed chairman and asked to raise the necessary talent. While in the process of doing this I came across a woman whom I had met before in India. She had previously been married to a colonel in the Sappers, but had recently been divorced. There had been quite a lot of scandal about it in the papers as the husband, as the innocent party, had named co-respondents running into double figures!

I asked the divorcee if she would care to do a turn at the concert.

"Well," she said, "when we get to Marseilles I'm going to Paris to practise my old profession."

I must admit that, knowing her reputation, I sort of sniggered at this remark and she retorted: "Oh no! Not that. I'm a professional dancer."

I told her this would be ideal and that we would be delighted if she could give a show at the concert, which she agreed to do.

The night of the concert arrived and suitably attired the divorcee came on to do her turn. It was absolutely frightful. If one can imagine a camel dancing it would be about the nearest thing to this poor woman's effort at graceful entertainment. Of course, the audience was convulsed with laughter for all the wrong reasons, and kept bringing her back to encore after encore. After the fourth encore it became so embarrassing that I had to go backstage and explain that the audience was really only pulling her leg. It was all rather pathetic. Little did we know at the time what fate had in store for her, and that it was to be her last dance.

The last four days of the voyage were accompanied by a howling mistral and dense fog. The fog-horn boomed out day and night and we were thankful to reach Marseilles harbour. I lost no time in disembarking and getting onto my train. In the process I noticed several stretcher cases being taken off our ship, but didn't pay much attention to them at the time.

After a hot, stuffy, garlic-ridden journey through France I eventually got to England and made my way to my mother's place in the suburbs of London. Before leaving India I had ordered a new car — a Morris Cowley Continental it was called. As it was to be the first of this model to be exported to India, I was invited to go to Cowley near Oxford to take delivery of it. It turned out to be quite a ceremony with a lunch laid on and Sir William Morris (later to be created Lord Nuffield) personally handing me the keys. Sir William was very proud of the car and said he thought it would be most suitable for conditions in India. If I had any trouble with it I was to contact him personally.

I proudly drove my new car back to London and suggested to

my mother that I take her on a motor tour round the west of England, as my wife had still not arrived in her trooper.

On the morning of our departure I drove the car round to the front of the house, and while I was waiting for my mother the newspaper arrived. On opening it I saw headlines about four inches high:

"SMALLPOX ON TUSCANIA — 5 DEAD, 35 CASES. Urgent need for vaccination."

Horrified, I shoved the paper under the seat so as not to worry my mother, and deliberated what to do next. It said in the paper that all passengers from the Tuscania must report immediately to their nearest health authorities.

I decided to wait until we got to Bristol where we were to spend the first night with my aunt.

That evening I took my young cousin to the film "Rose Marie." Foolishly I had read up the symptoms of smallpox before we left, and this particular strain was called confluent, the worst and most deadly type of the disease. During the film I developed all the symptoms until I was feeling so ill that I told my cousin I would have to go home, although I naturally didn't tell her what I suspected. I hardly slept that night, and at first light the next morning I crept out of the house and went off to the nearest military hospital. When I got there I was met by a sergeant in the R.A.M.C. who greeted me.

"Good morning Sir. What can we do for you?"

"Well," I said, "I've got smallpox."

"Have you?" he said. "Well, you'd better wait for the M.O."

Within a short time a young medical officer arrived and I was asked again what the trouble was, to which I gave the same reply: "I've got smallpox."

I then told him about the Tuscania and all the casualties and deaths, and that I myself had all the symptoms of the disease. After he had examined me he asked me when I had left the ship. I told him that it was about twelve days previously. The M.O. then said: "Well, whatever you've got, it's not smallpox, the incubation period is ten days."

He asked me where I was going, and told me to report again at the military hospital at Exeter, just in case.

However, within minutes of leaving the M.O.'s office my "symptoms" had disappeared and my mother and I carried on with our tour with no further anxiety.

I subsequently saw in the newspaper that the unfortunate divorcee dancer had contracted the disease and died in Paris.

My wife eventually arrived at Southampton in her troopship, having had the most hectic three weeks. She became known throughout the ship as Paddy, on account of being Irish, and the C.O. of the ship handed her over to me saying: "We've looked after Paddy. She's in good running order!"

We spent eight months in England and Ireland, visiting our families and friends, and travelled everywhere in my new Morris Cowley.

I noticed that it seemed to be over-heating a bit, and I reported this when I handed it back to the Morris people for shipment to India. They said there was no real problem and it could be easily adjusted. The next time I saw the car was on the Bombay docks.

While on leave I received confirmation of my transfer to the Indian Army so that my wife and I immediately became eligible for free first class passages by P. & O. line on our return to India.

17

Trekking in Chamba

On arrival at Bombay I was posted to Lahore, capital of the Punjab. We loaded up the Morris and boiled our way to Lahore, some twelve hundred miles away, spending four nights on the way. I never managed to get the over-heating problem solved and my new car became known as the Field Kitchen. I finally wrote to Sir William, reminding him of his promise, and back came a reply saying that his representative would be coming to India in due course and would call on me. When he arrived I took him for a short run downhill and then turned to go back.

"Oh, it won't boil in this short distance," said the rep.

"Just you wait and see," I replied.

Sure enough, within a very short time steam started to pour out of the bonnet, much to the rep's surprise and embarrassment. He then promised that Morris would send a new engine out, but in actual fact all they did was to send out a modified cylinder head. This didn't help at all and at the first opportunity I got rid of the Field Kitchen and bought an American car which I found much more suited to the conditions in India.

The cantonment for Lahore was called Mian Meer. The name had been changed from Lahore some years before as it had such a bad reputation in Britain among the troops from a health point of view. In fact, it became so bad that British troops had been known to desert rather than be sent to Lahore.

However, things had improved considerably by the time we went there and malaria was well under control. The city itself was the scene of great social activity, being the seat of government for the Punjab. It also had many associations with the famous poet and author Rudyard Kipling who, in his youth, had been a reporter on the Civil and Military Gazette. The famous Kim's Gun — Zam Zama — was sited in the middle of the town.

The nearest hill station to Lahore was Dalhousie, some hundred miles away and about six thousand feet above sea level. When I got my first leave after returning to India I decided to go off into the Himalayas on a shoot, with the object of bagging a red bear. The nearest place to Dalhousie where one could hope to do this was a small independent state called Chamba, in which there was very good shooting. So I applied and got my permit which entitled me to shoot in an area or block about fifty miles square.

It was some fifteen miles from Dalhousie to the town of Chamba, capital of the small Himalayan state, about three hours walk.

Organising the expedition needed quite a lot of homework and forward planning, as it was not possible to buy anything once we left the town of Chamba. I took two tents, masses of tinned food, rifles, a quantity of ammunition, medical supplies and lots of a cheap brand of cigarettes. The latter were used as small tips for the *shikaris* and porters along the way. All this stuff was carried by porters down a track from Dalhousie to Chamba where the final arrangements were made, and where I bought my fresh produce for the trip, which was intended to last about a month and involved a trek on foot of about 200 miles in all.

I spent one night in a *dak* bungalow in Chamba, and managed to make all the necessary arrangements. This involved the hiring of some twelve ponies with porters to guide them. The pack animals and men would only travel one stage of about fifteen miles to the next village, when they would return home and all the stuff would be transferred to a new team. The most important member of the expedition was the *shikari* or hunter. I managed to get hold of a first-class fellow called Kumla, who brought his son along to help, and one personal porter who was with me the whole time.

Along with the fresh food that I bought in Chamba I managed to get hold of about two dozen live chickens which we took along in a basket. These we killed off as required. In another special basket we took some eight dozen eggs. In this way I felt sure that if the worst came to the worst and we weren't able to shoot anything for the pot, we would be able to survive for a month. Another important person was the *khansamah,* or cook. I don't think he'd have got a job at the Ritz, but he was good enough for our purposes.

My wife originally was to have come along on the trip, but when it was discovered that most of the journey was to be on foot she wisely backed out. She could never have stood up to the altitude and long climbs. However, a young officer friend of mine in the Scots Fusiliers was very keen to join me. He had done no shooting of this kind and had to borrow a sporting rifle. As no two sportsmen were allocated to the same "block," my friend was given another one, only two days march out of Chamba. This area was not likely to produce a red bear as the altitude was too low. My friend was always known as Witless, for obvious reasons, and to this day I can't remember his proper name.

I went and made the acquaintance of the British Resident, a colonel in the Indian Army, and told him what I was proposing to do and where we were heading.

Next morning at the crack of dawn the column moved off. The first two days were comparatively effortless as there was quite a wide track, which made the going fairly easy. We followed the course of the river Ravi, which has its source high in the Himalayas beyond the state of Chamba.

After two days Witless and I parted and he went off to his block accompanied by his *shikari* and a number of porters. I advised him to get in a bit of practice with his borrowed rifle, explained to him that I was heading for the village of Bahmour, and asked him to get in touch with me by runner if he was in any trouble.

The villages were spaced at roughly fifteen mile intervals, and were really staging posts. On arrival at the village the ponies or porters dumped their loads and a new set of ponies or porters were produced. After two days travelling it was impossible to make use of ponies owing to the roughness and inaccessibility of the terrain, and porters were used for the rest of the trip.

At each of these villages there was a headman or *lumbadar*. He would organise the porters for the next stage, and while the swap-over was being carried out, he would invite me into his house and give me thin-skinned walnuts washed down by a lethal brew known as *arrack*. The latter was made from fermented rice mixed with raw sugar. This potent mixture was guaranteed to blow your head off at one gulp, and I had been warned against it before leaving India. I made the excuse that having recently been injected for cholera I wasn't allowed to drink alcohol!

The Rajah of Chamba had thoughtfully provided chalets for travellers at intervals along the route. These were a godsend as they provided facilities for. cooking and sleeping, and saved pitching tents.

After the first two days the going became pretty rough, and the track became practically non-existent in parts. At some places on the steep mountainside the path had been eroded away. In order to overcome this difficulty horizontal beams had been driven into the hillside, with planks laid across them on which to walk. These deviations were about twelve yards long, with no handrail, and below you was a drop of several thousand feet. All pretty hair-raising and no place for ponies or those without a head for heights.

Where we had to cross ravines rope bridges had been constructed. These had to be crossed with care and would swing violently, even though you broke step. But at least they had handrails.

In between the many natural hazards I would stop and admire the magnificent scenery. Although we were below the snowline the peaks all round were covered. The bird life was extensive, with golden eagles, sunbirds, and occasionally a monal pheasant. Apart from peacocks, which abounded in the plains of India, these monal pheasants were quite the most beautiful birds I'd ever seen. About the same size as the European pheasant, they had a terrific wing-span, and when seen swooping down a hillside, rather like a fighter aircraft diving, a large white triangle could be seen in the middle of the back. The rest of the plumage was an irridescent

134

greenish blue, with a patch of red on the tail. These birds were regarded as sacred in Chamba and for that reason were protected game.

In this sparsely populated area there was also an abundance of wild flowers, among them rhododendrons and azaleas. Butterflies were much in evidence, each wing being the size of a small human hand. In fact, the whole area was a naturalist's paradise.

From the time that Witless and I parted until I got back to Chamba I never spoke a word of English, apart from a meeting with a brother officer on one of the rope bridges. He was serving with one of the Dogra regiments and was on his way back to India after a shooting trip.

Each evening after we had pitched camp old Kumla would make me lie down and would rub me all over, massaging and manipulating me from stem to stern. While he was doing this he would recount stories of the many hunting expeditions he had been on during his long career as a *shikari*. They were all told in picturesque Hindustani, and his soothing voice, together with the massage, had the most relaxing effect on me after a long day's arduous trek.

Some days we would climb up to ten thousand feet and then descend three thousand feet to a river valley and climb up the other side. Old Kumla would say "Slowly, slowly, and bend your knees" when we were climbing. But I must say that I was very lucky as the altitude never affected me, and I was able to cope as easily as the locals.

At the various villages where we used the chalets the local population would come streaming in to ask for some form of medication. They seemed to think that every white man was a sort of itinerant M.D. and a curer of all diseases. I had brought along quantities of aspirin, iodine and laxatives, known in the army as Number Nines.

Most of the ailments from which they suffered seemed to respond to one of these three, so that by the time I returned to the same villages they were all waiting for another dose. If none of my "cures" helped the ailment, I found that a packet of cigarettes was a panacea for all ills. In fact, I overheard one of them say: *Doctor Sahib wapas argia.* (The doctor has come back!)

After the best part of a week's climbing, with the going getting progressively worse we reached the village of Bahmour. This was the largest village in the state apart from Chamba itself. Here we rested for a day in one of the chalets, and then moved into the area in which I had been given permission to shoot.

We moved up to our base camp at about ten thousand feet the following day and pitched our tents on a small plateau. By this time the party consisted of Kumla, his son, one porter and a cook. They slept in one tent and I slept in the other. They managed to cook on an open fire, using brushwood for fuel.

That evening Kumla and I planned our shoot for the next day, and at first light we started off. We climbed to about twelve thousand feet looking for red bear. We saw quite a lot of *ghural, thar,* and rock pigeons by the hundred, but no sight or sign of a *lal balu* (red bear). We spent about four hours on the mountain enjoying the panoramic scenery and all the flora and fauna, and then returned to camp. We repeated this operation on two successive days, but still no sign of a bear. In fact, I really began to wonder whether there were any in my block.

On the evening of the third unsuccessful day old Kumla appeared at my tent carrying a small kid goat in his arms.

"Sahib," he said, "we've got to do something about getting a red bear. I think we ought to offer this up as a sacrifice, and perhaps the Gods will look kindly on us and produce one."

"All right," I said, "we've had no luck so far — anything's worth trying. How much do you want for the kid?"

"Oh, five rupees, Sahib," he replied.

So I gave him the money, and old Kumla withdrew with the kid. Personally I don't think he sacrificed it, or even killed it. I think he had some arrangement with one of the local shepherds and they probably went fifty-fifty.

Next morning at about three o'clock we started our climb once again. This time we were full of hope. We climbed up to about twelve thousand feet and I sat down with my back against a huge rock, while Kumla went off on a "recce". The sun was just coming up although it was pretty cold, with snow still lying in the shady hollows. I became so absorbed in the beauty all around me that I had almost forgotten about the red bear.

Suddenly the silence was broken by the calling of a bird called a *chikore*. For the moment I was nonplussed as this bird wasn't usually found at such a height. Then it suddenly dawned on me that this was the pre-arranged signal between Kumla and me should he wish to attract my attention. I looked in the direction of the noise, and there, about fifty yards away, was old Kumla pointing to a spot behind the rock where I was sitting. I got up and cautiously peered round the edge of it. There, to my absolute amazement, about fifteen yards away, was a magnificent *lal balu* or red bear. I just couldn't believe it, and I knew other people wouldn't either, so I thought I would try to photograph it.

Although the wind was in the right direction and bears normally have rather poor sight she appeared to be getting rather restive. So I decided that I'd better bag my bear while I could, as I might never get a chance like this again. She was standing up on her hind legs when I drew a bead on her, fired two shots and down she went. Kumla joined me and together we went to inspect our bear. She was a beautiful specimen, with a fine golden red coat. I felt rather sad seeing her lying there, but I was very keen to have red bear as a trophy, as they were rather rare.

While we were still admiring my trophy another red bear appeared, coming down the hill towards us hell for leather. He was making a great din and was obviously very angry and bent on attacking us. I realised that he was the male who had come to avenge his mate's death. When he got within a few yards of us I felt that it was going to be his life or ours, so although I had no wish to shoot him I had no alternative but to do so. He presented me with a perfect target as he came up on his hind legs between the rushes. I now had two red bears instead of the one permitted by my licence.

At this juncture old Kumla started wailing at the top of his voice: "Oh! Sahib, you are not ALLOWED to shoot two red bear, you're only allowed to shoot one."

"Yes, but that bear would certainly have killed us," I replied.

"But you are not allowed to shoot more than one, and I will get into big trouble when we get back to Chamba," Kumla wailed.

I told him that he was being ridiculous to make such a fuss and that I would fix it with the Colonel Sahib when we got back to Chamba. This appeared to pacify him to some extent.

However, our troubles were not yet over. Believe it or not, we were still arguing over my latest victim when two more bear appeared. These were youngsters, about three feet high, snarling and growling in a most menacing fashion. They were obviously the cubs of the pair I had shot and were even more aggressive than their parents. They kept rushing at us like savage dogs. I obviously didn't want to shoot any more bear, having already exceeded my allowance by one, so I decided that the only thing to do was to try and frighten them away. They were standing in front of a biggish rock, so I fired just to the left of them in order to hit it. Small splinters of rock must have hit them, and this plus the noise of the rifle was sufficient to frighten them away. They bounded off down the side of the mountain.

I said to the old *shikari:* "Do you think they'll be all right?"

"Oh yes, Sahib, they'll be all right. They're practically fully grown, they can look after themselves."

So we then got down to the business of the two bears that I'd shot. Old Kumla said that he couldn't agree to skin the two bears and I must decide which one I wanted. We decided on the first one — the female — who had the better coat of the two, and we buried the other one. We then sent the skin back to India with a porter with instructions to have it cured.

On the way back to our camp I put up a couple of little *ghural,* a small species of antelope rather like an Alpine chamois. By this time both the porters and I were in need of meat, so I decided to follow them up. When I got near them I fired a shot which missed but had the effect of stopping them.

They looked round to see where the noise had come from, which gave me the opportunity of shooting them, so that night we had fresh meat for dinner for the first time since we had left Chamba, much to the porters' joy.

That night in camp Kumla and I discussed the plans for the following day and he suggested that we should go and have a look for *thar,* a type of mountain goat. A magnificent-looking creature with a shaggy coat and a long beard, he stands about three feet high with short straight horns. These *thar* live in a very inaccessible part of the mountains, with sparse vegetation on which to feed.

During the night the old *shikari* made me a pair of plaited grass *chuplies* or sandals. These were worn over my own leather *chuplies* in order to give a better grip on the terrain and also to enable one to make little or no noise when walking.

The morning came and we started. We had been going for a short distance when I noticed that Kumla the *shikari* had taken up a position directly in front of me, with his son immediately behind me. The two porters were positioned on either side of me, the four of them thus making a diamond formation. I said to the *shikari:* "What's this in aid of?"

"You'll see Sahib, when we come to the place," he said.

Very shortly we came to an area which we had to cross. It was practically a precipice, with a drop of about three thousand feet. Feeling exactly like a fly on a wall, we started to cross this hazardous bit of mountainside. I must admit that I was terrified, and after a short distance I lost my nerve, and like a fool I tried to run for it. Of course then I realised what the formation that these chaps had taken up was for. They obviously anticipated this behaviour and closed in on me and held me down.

If it hadn't been for their prompt action I'm sure I'd have been "a gonner."

When I'd recovered my breath I said to the *shikari:* "I don't think I can go on with this. I don't mind climbing mountains, but this is a sheer precipice. We'll have to go back."

"No Sahib," old Kumla replied, "you must go on. If you stop now you'll never shoot in the Himalayas again."

Well, after resting for a time I finally got my nerve back and on we went. The terrain improved a bit and we reached the area where the *thar* were located. Across the valley we could see a herd of them — there must have been a hundred or more — about four hundred yards away.

We took up our positions and selected our possible trophy, a magnificent looking male standing up on a pinnacle of rock, silhouetted against the skyline. I fired and managed to hit him, but unfortunately he slipped as he fell and went down the precipice. We managed to recover the *thar* a couple of days later, but one of his horns had been damaged in the fall which spoilt him as a trophy. However, he provided a good meal for the porters who didn't mind the strong taste.

Of course the moment I had fired the shot the rest of the herd had disappeared into the blue, and as it would have taken days to catch up with them again, we abandoned the *thar* project and returned to camp.

There were a number of shepherds in the vicinity looking after flocks of sheep and goats. It was customary in the hot weather to move their flocks up into the mountains away from the heat of the plains, and to where there was better grazing.

A couple of these shepherds came to our camp early one morning and complained that a black Himalayan bear was pinching their lambs. They asked me if I could help them by killing the bear. Having been given a rough idea of where he was located we set off to search for him. After a couple of hours of looking in the area we suddenly spotted the black bear. He was a huge fellow coming down one of the hilly features opposite at a terrific rate. I said to the *shikari*: "Come on, let's cross this bit of a valley here and head him off."

Well, we had to get a move on in order to do this, and I was down the valley and up the other side even quicker than the *shikari* and the porters.

"Oh Sahib, you mustn't go as fast as that, you'll burst your heart," said old Kumla.

We waited for some time for the bear to appear, but nothing happened, so we started to walk up the side of the hill hoping to meet him. Eventually we came to a cave and I said to the *shikari:* "I bet a quid he's in there."

I then suggested that the *shikari* went into the cave while I waited outside. Then, presuming that the bear would pursue old Kumla out of the cave, I would shoot it as he came out. However, Kumla didn't think this was a very good idea, and I can't say I blamed him. I then suggested that he take my revolver to protect himself in case the bear attacked him. Kumla thought this was a much better idea, so in he went while I waited outside on the alert and ready to shoot the old *balu,* the moment he appeared. However, after some time Kumla emerged and said: *Balu nahin hai.* (The bear's not there.)

Feeling that he must be in there somewhere, I went back into the cave with Kumla and we searched thoroughly, only to discover that there was another entrance to the cave on the other side, through which he'd obviously escaped. In fact, it was a tunnel going right through the hillside and not a cave at all. We searched the whole area for some time, but eventually had to concede that the bear had out-manoeuvred and outwitted us.

I had been wondering from time to time how Witless was getting on, and was pleased one day to see a runner appearing with a note from him. Apparently, soon after leaving me, he had taken my advice and gone out to try his borrowed rifle. He was wondering what to use as a target when what he described as "a furry object" appeared which he thought would be suitable. Firing a couple of shots at it, he subsequently discovered that he had shot a red bear. It seemed to be the most amazing instance of beginner's luck, as no red bear had been seen in that area for years. Of course old Witless was like a dog with two tails, and was delighted with his trophy. We didn't meet again until we were back in Dalhousie and were able to compare notes.

We were still installed at our camp near Bahmour and had been there about ten days when one night it suddenly started to pelt with rain. It was about three o'clock in the morning when the old *shikari* came into my tent and announced: *Sahib, Sahib, ye chota bursat argia.* (The little monsoon has started.) "We must think about getting back to Chamba in case the road gets washed away. If this happens we would have to go back via Simla, which would take weeks, and we haven't got enough food to last that long."

"All right," I said, "we'd better pack up and get across the Ravi before it comes down in spate."

We struck camp and got safely down to Bahmour and installed in one of the Rajah's chalets. That night, to my surprise, the rain stopped and the moon came out. I was looking out of the window admiring the peaceful scene, when I was amazed to see a hill leopard spring onto the basket containing the remaining chickens. I grabbed my rifle and fired a couple of shots, and of course all hell broke loose.

The chickens were squawking and terrified, and everyone came running to see what all the fuss was about. In the dark I had obviously missed the leopard, and discovered later that two of the chickens were missing. Whether it was the porters or the leopard who got them I never knew! Anyway, we'd managed to scare the leopard off and the rest of the night was peaceful.

Sure enough, the next night the rain came down harder than ever and I was satisfied that we'd made the right decision. We did, in fact, have quite a job getting across some of the bridges which had become waterlogged and even more hazardous. I think we were all quite pleased to see the town of Chamba again, and we had shortened the journey by two days.

I went to see the Resident in order to explain how we had come to shoot two red bear, in order to relieve Kumla's anxiety and clear his name as a conscientious *shikari*. The colonel said it was perfectly all right and that in the circumstances there was nothing else we could have done. He would have done the same himself. I asked him if he would talk to Kumla and explain that everything would be all right. This the colonel did and old Kumla left his office a much happier man.

I paid off and disbanded my entourage and proceeded up the winding track to Dalhousie. After nearly a month without shaving or having a haircut I had grown a woolly-looking ginger beard, a patchy moustache and my hair was flowing down over my collar. When I reached the hotel where my wife was staying she greeted me with the remark: "I thought you'd gone to shoot a red bear, but I see you've brought him back alive!"

18

People and places

Back in Lahore after our leave we had an unpleasant incident in the cantonments. I think it was really an aftermath of the Amritsar uprisings of 1919. These were instigated by a sect known as the Akali Sikhs, who had a religious feud with the Europeans. One of these Sikhs, carrying his traditional *kirpan,* a long curved sword, stealthily crept into the garden of the bungalow next to ours, where a nanny and three children were playing.

He then proceeded to attack the children with his sword. Both parents were out at the time. The nanny picked up the children and rushed into the house, but by then one child had been killed and the nanny injured. The father of the child, a British Army colonel, crazed with fury, had to be forcibly restrained from shooting the Sikh while he was in prison. However, the prisoner was eventually tried and hanged for murder.

India in those days seemed to abound in "characters" among the army people, and a few of them had some very unusual names, and also nicknames. Of course, we were all given nicknames by our Indian servants but mercifully we didn't all know what they were! One example of these was a chap called Hatt-Cook who was known to his servants and friends as *Topi-Khansamah,* just a literal translation in Urdu. Another fellow was called Sheepshanks, always known as the Wages of Sin on account of a rather debauched bachelor existence. Then there was Mrs. Bell-Chamber who was known as Tinkle-Jerry.

There was also a chap named Penrose-Welstead who became known as Feather Bedstead, and a Greek fellow by the name of Demisarkis who became Semi-Darkness.

At that time in India each province had its own British governor. As far as I remember the governor of the Punjab in 1930 was Sir Geoffrey Montmorency. The social life of Lahore centred round Government House. During the winter season there was always a ball, a garden party and a formal reception at which all officers and their wives were presented to the Governor and his Lady.

The ball was the most glittering affair of the whole season. Apart from the military guests and their wives, all the important people in the Indian Civil Service and prominent Indians from all walks of life attended. The Indian women in their traditional and magnificent Benares saris, many of them embroidered with real gold or silver thread, and studded with precious stones, really stole the show. Their husbands, in some cases maharajas or rajahs of states in the Punjab, would also be dressed in traditional garb, wearing their various orders and insignias. Their turbans would often be embellished by a large precious stone, such as an emerald.

The European women guests were turned out as befitted the occasion, and my wife was always in the forefront of the latest fashion, thanks to the local *dersi* or tailor. These chaps were amazingly talented in copying any sort of garment or illustration from a fashion magazine. In fact, they were so meticulous and exact in their reproductions that it became quite ludicrous on occasions. One chap I knew sent an old Saville Row suit to the local *dersi* to be copied. When the new suit arrived he found they had even reproduced the original maker's label and a darn in the seat of his pants!

A feature of the ladies' ball ensembles in those days were the beautiful fans they carried. These were extremely useful, as well as being ornamental. Many of them were embellished with ostrich feathers or embroidered with sequins or lace. The frames were made of ivory or tortioseshell. All the ladies wore long white gloves, which extended above their elbows and were fastened with tiny buttons.

So it was that India's high castes and V.I.P.s mingled and danced with the Sahib Log. Under the iridescent chandeliers in the palatial ballroom we danced until the early hours of the morning, refreshed by numerous *chota pegs* (small whiskies) and a sumptuous buffet supper. Those were the days never to return; the British Raj was at its height.

During the winter in Lahore there were endless social events. Dances every Saturday at the club, gymkhanas, race meetings, polo tournaments and so on.

Despite this apparently endless round of pleasure, strenuous training and manoeuvres were carried out, involving absence from Lahore for weeks on end.

In 1931, after a two-year stint in Lahore I was sent to Rawalpindi District H.Q. as Deputy Assistant Director of Ordnance Services. This was a four-year appointment, and a very pleasant job indeed. No more hot summers on the plains as the H.Q. staff moved en masse to Murree in the hills. There was also a very limited amount of touring so that I was able to enjoy much more home life than I had before.

The General Officer Commanding of the district was called Findlayson, known as Copper Findlayson because of his ginger hair. He was an ex-gunner and British Service. He and I got on very well together and thanks to him I was awarded a Brevet Majority which improved my prospects considerably.

During my period on the District Staff I was given the job of going to Abbottabad with several brother officers, forming a board. The assignment necessitated going to each Gurkha battalion and assessing the condition of their equipment and so on to enable the government to compensate them financially. Previously the Gurkha regiments had been granted an annual amount of money to enable them to buy their own equipment. They were now being brought into line with the normal Indian Army procedure.

One of the battalions we had to assess was part of the Sixth Gurkha regiment. It was commanded by Bill Slim, who at that time was a lieutenant colonel. It was rather unfortunate that he tried to pass a lot of dud equipment off onto us. It was absolute rubbish and as it was quite worthless we rejected it.

When I made out my report after completing the assessment on return to Rawalpindi, I handed it to General Copper Findlayson. In my report I regrettably had had to make some rather derogatory remarks about Bill Slim and his equipment. Soon afterwards the general sent for me and said: "Hodgson, do you realise what you are saying in this report?"

"Yes, Sir, " I replied.

"Are you prepared to stand by what you have said?"

"Absolutely Sir," I affirmed.

"Well," he said, "you know that if it's proved to be untrue, you'll run the risk of getting into very serious trouble."

"Well Sir," I said, "that's my opinion and I will stand by it."

So the general, turning to his adjutant quartermaster, who was a colonel, said: "Ring Abbottabad and ask Colonel Slim to come here as soon as possible."

Well, as Abbottabad was some seventy miles away Bill Slim didn't arrive until the following morning.

I was waiting in my office, and by this time was beginning to feel pretty nervous about the whole thing. Anyway, it was too late for regrets and I just had to face the music.

Suddenly my phone rang and the A.Q. said: "The general would like to see you."

Down I went to the general's office with my knees knocking, and there standing talking to the general was Colonel Bill Slim. As I walked towards them Bill turned to me and said: "Hello Hodgson. You were perfectly correct in what you said in your report, and I admire you for having the courage of your convictions. You were entirely correct in taking the action you did and I apologise for any trouble I may have caused."

"I'm sorry too, Sir," I answered, "but I felt I had to do what I considered to be my duty."

Bill Slim then shook me by the hand and we had a bit of general conservation. At this time I was only a captain, and this incident made me realise what a fine character Bill Slim was, both as a soldier and as a man. This was to be confirmed many times during the next fifteen years, as our paths crossed in the course of duty.

During my travels in India I had some interesting and amusing experiences.

On one occasion I was driving from Rawalpindi to Campbellpore accompanied by my orderly, Mohamed Ali. We were rattling along when we were flagged down by an Indian standing in the middle of the road. I stopped and asked him what the trouble was, and he told me that he was a *tonga wallah* (driver of a small horse-drawn trap). He said his pony had broken its leg. He led me across the road to where his tonga was ditched, with the poor pony lying pathetically on its side, still in the shafts. Knowing a good deal about horses I examined the pony, and sure enough it had broken one of its forelegs. The *tonga wallah* implored me to shoot it and put it out of its pain. I went back to the car, got my revolver and asked Mohamed Ali to come back to the *tonga* with me so that he could witness the fact that the man was asking me to shoot his pony.

I was very reluctant to shoot a rather nice animal, but it had to be done, and luckily I had been taught at Weedon how to perform this unpleasant task. There is a special place on the forehead where the bullet must penetrate, and done this way death is instantaneous and painless. I commiserated with the *tonga wallah* on the loss of his pony and continued my journey.

A couple of months later I got a summons to appear in court, on a charge of "Wilfully destroying a *tonga wallah's* pony." The plaintiff was claiming the cost of the pony from me.

I was naturally furious about this. Having done the man a favour he was now trying to double-cross me. I had to attend the court, so I took my orderly with me.

The proceedings opened and I found myself charged with not only destroying his pony, but depriving him of his livelihood as well. When it was my turn to give evidence I told the Indian magistrate the true version of the story which was, of course, corroborated by my orderly.

The magistrate then said: "This puts a very different complexion on the case. The charge against you will be withdrawn."

The *tonga wallah* was then charged with making a false accusation and was punished accordingly. Luckily for me, I had my orderly with me in the car, or it would have been my word against the *tonga wallah's*. However, this experience made me very wary of getting involved in matters like this in the future.

On another occasion I was doing one of my inspection stunts, also accompanied by Mohamed Ali. It is self-evident that he was a Muslim by religion. As we were driving along a little country road a sounder of wild pig suddenly shot across the road. There was a sow with seven piglets in file. I slowed up to let them pass, and they disappeared into the jungle on the other side of the road. I happened to look at Mohamed Ali who was sitting next to me, and saw that he had completely covered his face with his *puggery* (turban). I spoke to him in Hindustani and said: "What's the matter with you, Mohamed Ali?"

Suer . . . suer, he replied, *bahut karab,* meaning "pig . . . pig, very bad."

Then I remembered that to a Muslim a pig is so unclean that even to see one is abhorrent to them. As soon as we got to our destination my orderly immediately went off and washed himself in order to purge any contamination.

At about the same time I had a Muslim cook. When we had bacon for breakfast old Fazil Ali would get one of the non-Muslim servants to put the bacon in the pan and put on a lid. He would then cook the "unseen" bacon, and once cooked the other servant would "unveil" it and bring it to the table!

Fazil Ali used to do all the shopping. He would go off to the bazaar in the early morning and buy all the fresh food we required for the day. After breakfast he would bring the shopping list to my wife and read it out to her. One day I was present when this was taking place so I had a look at his list. The first item he had written was "foul," which had been crossed out and the word "kok" substituted. This had also been deleted, and the final result was "hen."

Passing through an Indian village one day an old man stopped me and asked if I would give him a lift to the next village, some ten miles away. I said: "OK, get in."

But the man said that he would sit on the running board of my open tourer. He got on and with his left hand hung on to the top of my door.

Tik hai, Sahib, (all right) he said and off we went.

I asked him to let me know where he wanted to get off and he said he would. As we got near the village I had begun to slow down, when I heard the old man say: *Meri bani Sahib,* meaning "Thank you very much."

Whereupon he just stepped off the running board while the car was still travelling at forty miles an hour. He hit the road with a terrific thud and rolled over and over. I slammed on the brakes and screeched to a halt, thinking that the old chap must have broken his neck.

However, I was very relieved, on looking back, to see him sitting up in the middle of the road. I backed the car, and on coming abreast of him, asked if he was all right, and why on earth he hadn't asked me to stop. He replied that he was quite all right and that he hadn't wanted to give my any further trouble. Of course he had probably never been in a car before and had no idea of the speed. Their usual mode of transport was a *tonga* or a bullock cart.

I remember once in Calcutta I was having tea on the verandah of an hotel overlooking a crowded street. Presently a poor, starving, emaciated Hindu woman carrying a baby on her back stopped and raised her hands imploringly towards me, saying: *Gharib parwar* (defender of the poor), a term often used by begging Indians.

I had no money on me at the time so I cut off a large piece of cake and handed it to her. She thanked me effusively, walked away and threw the cake into the street. I then realised that being a white man I had contaminated the cake, and that though starving she wouldn't eat it. However, she was too polite to refuse. A people with customs that appear strange to us.

In those days relations between ourselves and the Indian people were excellent, particularly among the country folk. I was out for an early morning gallop and riding along a path in between some crops. Coming towards me was an elderly Indian riding a donkey and holding an umbrella over his head. As we drew close we hailed one another and the old Indian solemnly dismounted, folded his umbrella and bowed right down until his forehead touched the ground. He wasn't being obsequious, it was merely his traditionally polite form of greeting and indication of friendliness. He then greeted me with the usual Indian salutation: *Salaam, Sahib bahadur. Gharib parwar.*

We then had a short conversation about his farm and crops and other general matters. It was then my place to indicate that the talk was over, as by custom he would not have terminated it himself. So I said: *Accha gi, Salaam,* — roughly translated meaning, "all right, goodbye."

The old boy remounted his donkey, put his umbrella up to protect himself from the fierce sun, and away he went. I galloped off and completed my morning's exercise.

It was customary, when engaging servants in India, for them to produce a reference, or *chitti.* On one occasion I was engaging a sweeper, whose main task was to deal with the sanitation side of the establishment. I asked him if he had a *chitti,* and he proudly produced one signed by General Uniacke, who was then the district commander. It read as follows:

"Budloo has been my sweeper for the last year. I can thoroughly recommend him. He takes a morbid interest in his loathsome trade."

A short time later I was looking for a *kitmagahar,* or waiter. Strangely enough a fellow applied for the job who had also worked for General Uniacke. In this case the *chitti* was brief and to the point.

"Abdul Karim has been my *kitmagahar* for the last three months. Quothe the raven . . .!"

One day, my bearer, a Kashmiri, asked me if he could have ten days' leave as his wife was expecting a baby. After ten days I received a telegram from him asking for his leave to be extended, saying: "The hand that rocks the cradle has kicked the bucket."

19

Tribal ops

During my time in 'Pindi as D.A.D.O.S. I became very friendly with a chap called Bobby Erskine of the 60th Rifles, a British regiment doing its tour in India. They were brigaded with the Rawalpindi Brigade which consisted of themselves and two Indian regiments.

Bobby Erskine was the brigade major and he and I had a lot of official contacts. One day he asked me if I would dine with him in the 60th Rifles' Mess. I considered this a bit of an honour as it was one of the crack infantry regiments of the British Army and was regarded as being rather snobbish.

Dressed up in my mess kit I went along on the appointed evening to dine. I found all the officers of the 60th Rifles were dressed in mess kit but none of them was wearing badges of rank. They were all introduced by their Christian names so that you didn't know whether you were talking to the Colonel or the last-joined subaltern. Introductions over, Bobby then asked me what I would like to drink.

I said: "A *chota peg,* please."

"What did you say?" he asked.

"I said a *chota peg.*"

"What's that?" he asked.

"Surely you know what it means," I replied. "It's Hindustani for a small whisky and soda."

"Oh, we never speak that language in the mess," he retorted. However, I got my *chota peg* all the same!

Talking to officers of the Indian regiments I found that none of them had ever been asked to dine in the 60th Rifles' Mess. Apparently they had never mixed socially. Considering that they were brigaded and had to fight together I found this rather strange.

My friend Bobby Erskine eventually became a general, but his career was tragically ended during the last war when he went down with the H.M.S. Prince of Wales when it was sunk by the Japanese.

The chief pre-occupation of the British and Indian troops stationed on the North West Frontier was to prevent the tribes-men, whose activities were usually motivated by the prospect of loot, from invading India. In some cases this even ran to women, whom they used to abduct for the purpose of propagating the tribe. When the women had produced the offspring, preferably male, they conveniently disappeared. One very seldom saw women in the tribal territory.

The type of warfare carried out on the frontier was highly specialised, and troops had to be trained specially for it. The Gurkhas were some of the best people for this purpose as they were hillmen. It was really guerilla warfare.

The normal method of dealing with the tribesmen was to send a column into tribal territory. Because of the amount of equipment, food and ammunition necessary for such an expedition we had to stick to the valleys. This made the column an easy target for the tribal snipers in the hills on either side. They had the advantage of mobility with no transport problems.

They could travel for days carrying only a rifle, with ammuni-tion and food in a small pack slung over their shoulders, and they knew the country like the back of their hands. On occasion they would even attack the column itself, their prime targets being the ammunition-carrying mules and any small arms. Through years of experience in tribal warfare we found that the only way to cir-cumvent this was to picket the hills on the flanks of the column.

The punishment meted out to the tribesmen usually consisted

of burning their crops, destroying their houses and confiscating their cattle. At the conclusion of the campaign a *jirga* (conference) with the headmen was arranged by the civil authorities, and further punishment would be meted out by fining the tribesmen an appropriate number of rifles. In the old days they would depend on raiding to supply themselves with arms, but latterly managed to make some of their own. These were an exact replica of the 303. They were made in the Khyber Pass area and became known as Pass rifles.

The tribes of the North West Frontier consisted mainly of Pathans, Afridis, Mohmands, Masuds and Afghans. These in turn were divided into many sects, all disagreeing with one another. The only thing they appeared to have in common was making raids into Indian territory. This they did with great regularity, especially in the cold weather when they were short of food and the wherewithal to buy it. They even raided Peshawar, a big military cantonment, on one occasion.

A gruesome aspect of tribal warfare was the tribesmen's behaviour towards any of our troops taken prisoner or wounded.

For this reason we never left our dead or wounded in the area where we had been fighting if we had to withdraw. If any of our wounded fell into enemy hands their bodies would be mutilated by the tribesmen or their women. This was done by removing their private parts. The object behind this act of barbarism was that in their eyes we were infidels, and as such should be prevented from propagating our species.

The R.A.F. was a great help to us in these operations from a "recce" point of view. They flew over tribal territory in small planes, usually manned only by the pilot. They were generally armed with an automatic machine gun. These small planes, flying low, were comparatively easy targets for a sniper sitting on a mountain top, and they were occasionally shot down. The pilot, if captured alive, received the same ghastly treatment as our ground forces. In order to prevent this torture and to raise the morale of the pilots and the troops, large rewards were offered for the safe return of those captured, providing that they were returned "intact."

In 1935, while I was in Rawalpindi District H.Q., the Mohmands, who were normally a reasonably peaceful tribe, started to give trouble and threatened to invade India, so it was decided that we would send a force up into Mohmand territory to deal with the situation.

Subsequently a force was raised, delayed slightly by a shortage of the required number of camels. We had to have two thousand of these animals, which were needed to transport our tents, food, and ammunition, and were the most suitable means of transport for the rough and mountainous country. I accompanied the force as part of H.Q. staff, with General Findlayson in command.

We travelled north in a staff car via Attock, Nowshera and Mardan, and in due course met up with the Gurkha battalions from Abbottabad who were camped on the left bank of the Swat river at the Balambhat bridge. Our H.Q. was established in a *dak* bungalow high above the Swat river. Prior to our arrival the Mohmands had destroyed the Balambhat bridge, which for the moment prevented our crossing into their territory.

So our first job was to build a bridge across the river. A Bailey bridge was built by the sappers who were part of our force. Patrols which were sent into Mohmand territory had the effect of bringing the tribesmen to their senses and within a few days they sent a deputation down. They'd evidently decided that discretion was the better part of valour. So we agreed to talk to them and in the end a crowd of Mohmands came over the bridge to our side where we held a *jirga,* or big talk, which lasted for several days. After three of four days *bhat karroing* or talking, the tribesmen agreed to our terms. It was arranged that they should hand over a certain number of rifles by way of a fine.

I found it very interesting to meet and talk to these tribesmen. They were always very friendly, although I knew that they would shoot you the next minute without any compunction. They showed me their rifles of which they were very proud. They had about seven different makes, which I thought was a disadvantage from an ammunition point of view, but it didn't seem to worry them as, of course, they used what they could get or steal.

One morning while we were still camped at the Balambhat

154

bridge, I was driving down from our H.Q. with the general and as we looked down to the Gurkha tents camped below on the river bank, I said to him: "Look at those Gurkha tents, Sir. They appear to have camouflaged them. I wonder why?"

Instead of being their usual khaki colour they were almost black. The general agreed that this indeed seemed to be the case. However, when we got down into the camp we discovered that what we had taken for camouflage was in fact millions of flies. The early morning sun shining on the canvas had provided a warm place in which these *mukki* (flies) could bask.

The operation was finally concluded and the two Gurkha battalions withdrew and with the other troops started the week's march back to their base at Abbottabad. They hadn't been there very long when about eighty per cent of the battalions went down with malaria. Luckily it didn't happen while we were coping with the Mohmands.

The most distant and remote station that I visited in my inspection area was a place called Chitral, in the far north-west of Kashmir. It was about nine thousand feet high in the Hindu Kush range of the Himalayas, and very close to the Afghanistan border. I had to visit Chitral every two years, as we had a small garrison there.

A relief column used to go up there from time to time to take rations, ammunition and personnel replacements, so I organised to go up with the next relief column. We set out from a place called Malakand, which was about six days march from Chitral, along narrow mountain tracks. The supplies, etc., were carried by mules and porters. The scenery was most impressive and we had some marvellous views of Nanga Parbat which, at 26 000 feet, is one of Himalaya's highest peaks. The name means naked mountain, as it is always snow-covered.

We finally reached Chitral and got a great welcome from the British officers at the garrison who were delighted to receive news and supplies from the outside world. As radio in those days was not very efficient, and there was no contact by plane, they were completely isolated from civilisation between the relief column's visits, which came about once a month.

Having done my inspection and spent a couple of days loafing about, we set off down the track back to India.

As I was in the vicinity of the famous Khyber Pass I thought I would go and have a look at it. The valley up to the Afghan border was heavily fortified, but we managed to get there despite security. The Afghan sentries were much in evidence at the border and I managed to talk to one of them and examine his rifle, which was completely U.S. (unserviceable).

20

Back to school

My four-year appointment finished in 1935, and this seemed to be a good opportunity to take long leave in the U.K. as I'd only had one overseas leave since arriving in India in 1922. This time we could travel together first class on a P. & O. liner.

We embarked at Bombay, and on looking at the passenger list I saw the name Major H.L. Hodgson and wife, travelling in a de luxe cabin. This was my youngest brother, Leslie, and his wife Dodo. I knew he was in India at the time, but didn't know he was going on leave. So I went along to his cabin and found that he'd decided to chuck the army and take the special terms that the Indian Government were offering in order to reduce the number of superfluous officers. He fell on his feet on arrival in the U.K. when he got a job with B.S.A. Ltd. as liaison officer, and subsequently became a director in the firm. He was never cut out to be a soldier, as he wouldn't knuckle down to discipline.

The night before we left Rawalpindi on leave I was having a drink with a doctor at the club. During the course of conversation I mentioned the fact that I had a growth on my lower left eyelid. He looked at it and said: "When are you going on leave to England?"

"Oddly enough, I'm going tomorrow," I replied.

The Doc then got up and returned a few minutes later with an envelope. "Take this letter to Millbank Hospital and give it to Colonel Biggar," he said.

After a very pleasant voyage we arrived in London and off I went to the Military Hospital at Millbank. I got hold of Colonel Biggar and handed him the letter, and after he had read it he asked: "Can you come into hospital this afternoon?"

This rather shook me, as I didn't even know what was wrong with me.

Colonel Biggar said: "Well, you know what you've got, don't you? It's a rodent ulcer."

To cut a long story short, I had the rodent ulcer removed and was then sent to the Middlesex hospital for radium treatment. This took some time to heal and involved a subsequent medical board at the India Office. There it was decided that I was unfit to return to India and they kept extending my leave. This was all very well, but once having exceeded my eight months' leave I was put onto half pay, so we were pretty hard up.

After three extensions of my leave I told the board that I was going back to India and would take the consequences. The gentlemen on the board said that I was very unwise and would do so at my own risk, because of the climatic conditions.

So I booked our passage on the first available ship which was the Viminali, sailing from Trieste. We spent a short time in Switzerland en route to Italy and stayed at a little alpine village called St. Cergue near the French border where we enjoyed the winter sports of 1937.

We eventually boarded the Viminali at Venice, and from there sailed to Fiume on the Yugoslav/Italian border. There was a bit of a fuss going on at the time and a good deal of tension between the two countries owing to the fact that two Italian officers had been murdered by the Yugoslavs. In spite of this we were anxious to see the Yugoslav section of Fiume, and a party of us went ashore. We crossed the border without difficulty, but when the time came to return it was a different story. The whole party was detained at the border post and it looked as though we might miss our ship.

However, very luckily for us, there was an American professor in the party who could speak some Slav language that they could understand. Thanks to this and some financial persuasion they eventually let us back into the Italian section and we sailed for Brindisi.

Following the usual route via the Red Sea we called at Massawa in Italian Eritrea. There was a mixed crowd on board consisting of just about every European nationality. One chap was an Austrian who had just sold his factory and was feeling frightfully rich. He made up a party to go ashore and have dinner in Massawa. While we were waiting for the dinner to be served he asked the waiter if he could get us a bottle of whisky. Up to this point in the voyage our drinks had mainly been rather rough Chianti, and other wines, as no whisky was available on board. At this time the Fascist organisation was gaining great popularity and influence in Italy. Pictures of Mussolini hung in every public room in the ship and the crew greeted each other with the Fascist salute. Among the English-speaking passengers no reference was ever made to Mussolini by name. If necessary, we would refer to him as "Mr Smith!"

Our Austrian friend gave the waiter roughly the equivalent of ten pounds sterling in Italian money, as the whisky was presumably black market. When the waiter brought the bottle and the change my Austrian friend said: "Keep the change and give it to the Fascist Organisation."

We went back to the ship and spent a peaceful night, and at the crack of dawn the next morning the ship sailed. We had only moved a hundred yards off the quayside into the bay when a gun started to boom and the captain put on the handbrake. Almost immediately we saw a pinnace racing towards us. As it neared the ship we could see a couple of Italian police officers on board. They clambered up a rope ladder and disappeared into the captain's cabin. All the passengers were by now on deck and craning their necks to see what was going on, and there was much speculation and general excitement.

Several passengers were then summoned to the captain's cabin, among them our Austrian host of the night before. He eventually emerged waving a couple of bank notes and laughing, and then we heard what all the fuss was about.

Apparently the waiter who had been given the change and told to "give it to the Fascist Organisation" had been talking, and the story had been passed on to the Fascist authorities. The two Italian officers had been sent on board to return the money with the message: "Thank you very much, but the Fascist Organisation does not need any financial assistance from an outside source." It seemed unbelievable that they would go to all that trouble to actually stop a ship for the sake of a few pounds.

The old Viminali finally got under way again and we sailed down to Djibouti in Somaliland. All the dock workers there seemed to be Fuzzy-Wuzzies, or, correctly speaking, the Beggara tribe. They were huge coal-black fellows with this great mop of fuzzy hair. While in Djibouti we did a trip in a glass-bottomed boat. It was a wonderful experience looking at all the denizens of the deep. The water was crystal clear and we were able to see all kinds of vividly-coloured fish and coral.

Our part of the voyage ended in Karachi where we disembarked and proceeded to Rawalpindi once again. I was appointed to Northern Command H.Q. as assistant to the deputy director of Ordnance Services.

I had only been in this job for about six months when to my great surprise I was selected to go on a two-year course at the Military College of Science at Woolwich. The military minds work in a mysterious way and ours was not to reason why. So back we went to England on another P & O Liner, once again at government expense.

In due course I reported at the Military College to find myself the "Head Boy." There were twenty-four officers on the course and they came from those parts of the world which were friendly towards Britain. They included two officers from the Imperial Chinese Army, one each from Egypt, Malta, Canada, Australia, five from India, two from South Africa and the balance was made up from British officers in the U.K.

I was given a pep talk by the commandant in which he told me what policy I should adopt with such a mixed crowd of officers, stressing that Britain's prestige was at a low ebb and that I must use this opportunity to do everything I could to improve it.

The college was staffed chiefly by civilian professors, and the syllabus included maths, ballistics, manufacture of artillery pieces, TV and radio, the internal combustion engine and related subjects. Connected with the above were visits to military installations such as Woolwich Arsenal, a naval cordite factory, an underground ammunition storage depot near Bath, a vast vehicle depot situated close to Nottingham, a small arms school at Hythe and the anti-gas school at Porton.

The course involved pretty intensive study and hard work, and there was little time for sport and recreation, except at weekends. I think we all realised that war was inevitable and that this course was something which would prove invaluable in the future.

From my point of view the most essential part of the course was learning all about mechanical transport in order to bring about the mechanisation of the Indian Army. At that time we were still using camels, mules and horses for transport of equipment and for drawing the guns. In fact, when I first went to India in 1922 some of our guns were drawn by elephants. We had about a dozen attached to our battery and they were housed in an immense building, rather like an aeroplane hangar.

After about twelve months of intensive lectures and classroom work at Woolwich, we progressed to the more practical side of the course late in 1938.

In the meantime most of us found it pretty hard going, being older men and unaccustomed to this prolonged academic study. As "head boy" I was supposed to take an interest in the other students and help them where possible. One day, the commandant asked me how the two "Chinks" were getting on. I was able to tell him an amusing story about them.

During the morning break, after a particularly tough session of maths, I went down to the classroom and found the two Chinese still hard at work. So by way of opening a conversation I said to them: "How did you find the maths lecture this morning?"

To which one of the Chinamen replied, "Welly elementary!"

I had a look at their notebooks and found that they had copied every notice in the classroom including signs that said "Gents" and "Fire hydrant."

They were quite an amusing pair and used to travel about in a small Ford car, with one of them sitting in the back while the other drove. I asked them why they did this, thinking that it might be a question of social standing, that one might be a mandarin and the other not. They replied that this was not the case; it was a precautionary measure. If they had an accident the chap in the back was less likely to get injured! In fact, they did have an accident some time later when they crashed into an open-air vegetable stall. Apart from the car being plastered with all types of fruit and vegetables there was no real damage, but they had to compensate the stall owner.

We had one problem student in the form of a Captain Hafez from the Egyptian Army. I noticed a couple of times in class that he had dropped off to sleep, so I asked him one day how he was getting on. He replied that he wasn't getting on at all well as he really couldn't understand what half of it was all about. Could I suggest what he could do as it was imperative that he should pass the course. Having ascertained his standard of education I suggested that he should attend a night school. He thought this was a good idea but was worried about leaving his wife and child whom he had with him. I then suggested that he should send them back to Egypt so that he could concentrate full-time on his studies. He was agreeable to this, but asked me if I would talk to his wife. Mrs Hafez came along with him the next morning, a very smart and attractive woman, and she agreed whole-heartedly with my suggestion. She was prepared to do anything to further her husband's career, so she and the child packed up and returned to Egypt.

During the classroom work in vehicle maintenance a car was brought into the room. We were given a list of possible defects and told to assess the trouble. This done, the professor would check the list and detail a number of officers to get into dungarees and to put it right. Excellent training it was, and came in extremely useful when one's car packed up in some remote place.

One of our first visits was to the gun factory at Woolwich arsenal where we watched 16 and 20 inch naval guns being manufactured. At this time England was preparing for possible attack by aircraft flying at a great height which necessitated making up the tube or bore of the gun of specially hardened steel to withstand the high muzzle velocity.

Up to this time we had been making the "A" tube by the French method known as auto-frettage, but this only produced a tube capable of firing ten to fifteen rounds, after which the tube had to be replaced, making it somewhat impractical and cumbersome. This problem was solved in the most extraordinary way.

When Hitler invaded Czechoslavakia some half-a-dozen experts escaped and flew out from Skoda with a number of automatic weapons and the formula for making steel to the hardness required by the modern anti-aircraft gun. This obviated the necessity for frequent changes of the "A" tube and was of tremendous value to Britain's effort in the war. When the Czechs first arrived in Britain they were arrested as spies, until it was found that they were very pro-British.

The Czechs were invited to Hythe Small Army School to demonstrate their hardware. A machine-gun that fascinated me was one that was capable of firing nine hundred rounds per minute and was air-cooled, so that it hardly ever needed to have the barrel changed. This was an enormous advance on anything we had.

The next place of interest that we visited was an ammunition storage depot at Corsham near Bath. It was well below ground level and absolutely impervious to enemy bombing. It covered a very large area, having previously been a quarry from which the famous Bath stone was extracted. One of the main problems was to try and prevent fungus growing on the ammunition boxes as a result of the damp conditions. They had tried various types of paint, all to no avail, and the problem was finally solved by air-conditioning the entire place. Sufficient accommodation had been built to house all the staff and their families in the event of war.

From Corsham we went down to the south coast and were taken round the naval cordite factory and on to Reading where we stayed for some time at the Caversham Bridge Hotel. From here we visited the anti-gas school at Porton and many other military installations in the Aldershot district. We then went north to the army vehicle depot at Nottingham, where among other things we were taught to drive every vehicle from a motorbike to a tank. After our comprehensive tour of various other naval and military stations we returned to Woolwich to sit for our final exams.

Poor old Captain Hafez was in a terrible state — he was so afraid he wouldn't pass. However, when the results were announced he had got through by one mark. He was quite beside himself with joy and threw a huge party in a local hotel to celebrate, to which we were all invited.

By the time the course finished war was likely to be declared at any moment and the overseas members of the course couldn't wait to get out of England and back to their own countries. My wife and I managed to get passages on the ill-fated P & O liner Rawalpindi which sailed a few days after war was declared.

Her captain was a man called E.C. Kennedy whom we got to know quite well. Little did we realise that within two months the ship, her captain and most of the crew would be at the bottom of the sea.

On November 23, 1939, while on northern patrol as an armed merchant cruiser, the Rawalpindi was intercepted by the enemy battle-cruisers Scharnhorst and Gneisenau. In an heroic stand Captain Kennedy put up a gallant but hopeless fight and went down with his ship.

21

Destination Iraq

In due course we arrived in Bombay where I was to pick up a car which I had ordered in England. I had been posted to a place called Kirkee and it was a short drive across the Ghats mountains to our new station, where I was to take up an appointment as deputy chief ordnance officer of Kirkee arsenal. With the appointment went a very spacious bungalow and a pleasant garden.

The General Motors people met us on the docks with my new Chev car. We were then entertained to lunch by the general manager and they really gave us VIP treatment. After lunch they saw us off en route for our new home at Kirkee, about a hundred miles away.

After a short time a peculiar noise developed in the car, a sort of rattle. I stopped at several service stations en route but they could find nothing wrong, so we continued the journey and started the climb over the western Ghats. The noise continued, and when we reached one of the highest points, very luckily for us we got a puncture. The puncture actually saved our lives. When I got out of the car to change the wheel with the assistance of two passing Indians I jacked up the car and the wheel immediately fell off. On examination I found that the three other wheels were in the same state. The road at this point had a drop of about a thousand feet on our side, and had the wheel come off while we were moving I would almost certainly have lost control and the car would have gone over the precipice.

After recovering from the shock and making sure that the wheels were all secure we continued our journey to Kirkee and started to settle into our bungalow.

War had now been declared, and as my wife was hanging the last curtain I got a telegram from Army H.Q. "Proceed to join a division at Secunderabad." So off I went at practically a moment's notice to take up the post as deputy assistant director of ordnance services of the division. The G.O.C. seemed to be pleased to see me as he remarked: "At last I've got an officer with some knowledge and seniority."

Believe it or not, almost within hours of my arrival I received another telegram from Army H.Q.: "Proceed to Bombay and await orders."

So I took my leave of the G.O.C. who passed some unprintable remarks about Army H.Q. and took off for Bombay. I just had time to phone my wife and give her the news, and as the train was due to stop at Kirkee on its way to Bombay I suggested that she should be on the platform and I could explain everything while the train was in the station. However, it was not to be. Instead of stopping at Kirkee the train sailed through, leaving a forlorn-looking wife standing waving on the platform.

On arrival in Bombay I was told that my job would involve taking over the entire output of the Ford and General Motors Companies. We were to form a distribution depot at Colaba as part of the programme to mechanise the Indian Army. It was a very exacting but very interesting job. One of the best aspects of the assignment was that my wife was able to join me and that we were billeted at the Taj Mahal Hotel at government expense.

It was a truly magnificent place with every possible comfort, including air conditioning, which was something of a rarity in those days. In our bathroom was a sunken marble bath.

One morning at breakfast, sitting at the table with me was an officer in the American army, who introduced himself as Major Simpson. I laughingly asked him if he was any relation to the famous Mrs Simpson who became the Duchess of Windsor. He replied: "Yes, she was my wife," and promptly changed the subject!

Mechanisation proceeded apace and any number of units called every day to take delivery of their vehicles. What struck me the most was the very poor standard of driving among the Indian troops. As most of the units had to cross the Ghats mountains the drivers would put their vehicles into bottom gear and stay there. As a result of this many of the gear-boxes were destroyed before they were properly run in.

We suddenly received orders to despatch four hundred trucks and lorries to Somaliland where a campaign was being fought by the Allies against the Italians. A very antiquated ship was put at my disposal, but to get the vehicles from my depot to the docks presented quite a problem as we had very few drivers. However, the G.O.C. Bombay was most helpful and he ordered the immediate mobilisation of all civilian professional drivers in Bombay. It was quite a job loading all the vehicles onto the ship, which was unsuitable for this type of cargo.

Just as the ship was ready to sail I received orders to commandeer nine touring cars suitable for staff officers, one of them being intended for the general.

Down I went to the biggest motor firm in Bombay and requisitioned nine beautiful tourers, much to the delight of the salesman, as the army had to pay the normal price. The cars were then driven to the depot where they had to be camouflaged by daubing khaki paint all over their elegant bodywork. It was such a rush job that the labourers simply slapped the paint on with their bare hands. It was a heartbreaking sight.

The ship duly sailed and after a couple of days I received a telex message: "Please disconnect all batteries on vehicles." Luckily I had had this done.

What a complete waste of time, labour and money the whole operation was, because on arrival at the port, Djibouti I think, the British troops there were in retreat. Obviously they didn't need the vehicles, but they did need the ship on which to embark the men. All the vehicles were dumped into the sea to make room for the troops. Such is war.

After six months in Bombay organising the distribution of vehicles to the army I received orders to proceed to Ferozepore in the Punjab and mobilise two units to proceed overseas. I was told off the record that we were destined for Kuala Lumpur in Malaya. We were given a date by which we were to be ready. The men that I was given were completely untrainable in the time allotted, but as Kuala Lumpur was not at that time in the fighting area further training was to be given there. The two units consisted of about twenty-five Indian and white officers, with trained British and Indian N.C.O.s numbering about fifty. The rest were all Indian conscripted *sepoys,* about a thousand practically raw troops.

When we saw the men that we had been given as so-called "recruits" our hearts sank. They looked more like a lot of retired pirates! Most of them had never worn shoes, let alone army boots, and, as for rifles, they didn't know one end from the other. Physically they were in very poor shape and many of them had only just scraped through the medical exam. These were the men that I was supposed to turn into soldiers in two months' time, transport to some unknown destination and take into action against a well-trained and seasoned enemy. By this stage in the war the Indian Army had been doubled from its peacetime strength, so that only the "dregs" were left to draw on. However, this was war and we just had to make the best of what we'd been given.

Although the army grub wasn't luxurious, it was plentiful and nourishing and far better than the recruits were used to at home. This, plus hours of "square bashing", soon helped to improve their physique. Of course, with a physical improvement came a certain amount of mental alertness, but even so it was hard going, and such a lot of instruction was needed.

The men came from all parts of the Punjab, and from many different sects, both Hindu and Muslim. The Indian officers had the main task of organising their training, food and general well being. At the end of the two month period alloted to us they had certainly improved out of all knowledge, specially in appearance, and I began to feel that there was hope of turning them into something resembling *sepoys.*

168

On the prescribed date two trains were allocated to transport the units to Karachi. It was in the middle of the hot weather and the journey involved crossing the Sind Desert. I remembered reading about an expedition similar to ours crossing the desert by train in World War I. They had lost many men from heatstroke. Fortunately there was an ice factory in Ferozepore, so we loaded up as much ice as possible to keep the carriages cool. The journey took two nights and a day and we arrived in Karachi with no heatstroke casualties.

We were told to embark on a ship designated H.3, of which I was appointed officer commanding. There were seven ships in all in our convoy waiting to sail. I had been given sealed orders and whilst awaiting sailing time an embarkation officer came on board informing me that our sailing time had been delayed by twenty-four hours and asking me to return my orders.

He reappeared about two hours before sailing time with a fresh lot of orders, with instructions that they must not be opened until we had been at sea for twenty-four hours. I thought that there must have been a change of destination, and asked the embarkation officer where we were going. He said: "Sorry, I'm not allowed to tell you. You'll find out when you open your orders."

After we had been at sea for about six or eight hours I noticed that instead of going south we were going north. This made it obvious to me that wherever we were going it certainly wasn't Kuala Lumpur.

I made the acquaintance of the captain, a chap called "Spud" Murphy. I went up to the bridge and asked him where we were going, and although we'd been at sea for nearly twenty-four hours he refused to tell me, saying rather abruptly: "You've got your orders, haven't you. You'll know in due course."

So I went back to my cabin and I regret to say that I cheated and opened my orders. The envelope was covered with several seals which bore the insignia of the Chief of the General Staff India, and was addressed to the officer commanding Troops on Board S.S. H.3.

The orders were headed MOST SECRET and were dated April 30, 1941, and read as follows:

1. The troops under your command are detailed for service in Iraq.
2. The port of disembarkation will probably be Basra.
3. On arrival the troops will come under command of Major-General W.A.K. Frazer, C.B.E., D.S.O., M.V.O., M.C., commanding 10th Indian Division.
4. The paramount importance of avoiding any action which involves infringing the neutrality of Iran or which might be regarded as doing so will be impressed by you on all ranks under your command.

(Signed)
For the Chief of the General Staff.

All this *tamasha* was caused by a chap called Rashid Ali, the Prime Minister of Iraq, who was pro-German. He eventually bolted into Iran. Once again, as it turned out, the Almighty was on my side. After we had left India a new force was formed to go to Kuala Lumpur in our place. They were subsequently captured by the Japanese and spent years in a P.O.W. camp, many of them dying in the process.

I found that we were indeed heading for Basra to join a force there called the PAI Force, the letters standing for Persia and Iraq.

We continued on our voyage north and had been at sea about two days, when in the middle of the night, while I was sleeping in my cabin, the captain sent a message down asking me to go up to the bridge immediately. On reaching the captain's cabin he handed me a radio message which read: "Enemy raider attempting interception of convoy."

So I asked old "Spud" the location of the raider, and he replied that it was some four hundred nautical miles to our west, according to the message he'd received.

"Well," I retorted, "what on earth do you want to get me out of bed at this hour of the night when the raider hasn't got a chance of making contact for at least twenty-four hours?"

The captain said: "Apart from giving you the information about the raider, I want you to have boat drill immediately."

"Oh no!" I replied. "I'm sorry, you can't have boat drill at this time of the night. Half my troops are practically untrained and if I ordered boat drill now they'd all be jumping over the side in panic."

"Those are my orders," said the captain, "and unless they're obeyed I'll log you."

"You can do what you like," I replied, "but I'm not having boat drill now. What I will do is to have it at crack of dawn, and if it's not to your satisfaction by all means log me, whatever that means."

Well, after a little more unpleasant discussion "Spud" said: "Come on, let's have a drink."

"Well that's the first sensible thing you've said this evening," I replied.

So old "Spud" and I sat down and as far as I can remember we knocked back the best part of a bottle of whisky, by which time our relationship had mellowed considerably. The captain told me that his ship had recently been withdrawn from the Red Sea area where they had hell knocked out of them by enemy bombers. I realised then that this accounted for his recalcitrant attitude and the jittery state of his officers and crew.

Eventually I returned to my cabin and woke my adjutant, an R.A.F. officer recuperating after having been shot down, who was sleeping in my day cabin. Explaining the situation, I told him that we must put on a first class show or his C.O. would probably be "walking the plank" at dawn! At daybreak the alarm was sounded, the men went to their boat stations and everything went off like clockwork. The captain complimented us on the exercise and everyone relaxed.

Later that morning the captain said that it was my job to organise the defence of the ship. So I asked him what they'd got in the way of armament. He pointed to the blunt end of the ship where a gun was located. I took some of my officers who were also ex-gunners and we went to inspect the gun, which looked as though it had recently come out of the British Museum. I formed a gun crew and we fired a few practice rounds, but as it only had a maximum range of six thousand yards I felt that our chances against a modern German warship were practically nil, and that our fate would be that of the Rawalpindi should we be attacked.

When I was speaking to the captain later, I asked him, in the event of our ship being sunk, what our action should be. He replied: "Well, of course you and I go down with the ship."

"Like hell!" I answered. "You can do what you like, but I'm not going down in an old tub like this."

"Incidentally," I asked him, "what's happened to our naval escort?" This was an Australian cruiser called H.M.A.S. Ballarat.

"Oh! She's gone off to try and intercept the German raider," he told me.

We practised boat drill several times during the day to take our minds off possible attack by the raider. I realised that we would be sitting ducks for any enemy ship as our convoy passed from the Gulf of Oman into the Persian Gulf. Late that evening the captain received another radio message. This said: "German raider engaged and sunk by H.M.A.S. Ballarat."

Cheers went up as the news went round the convoy, and with a sigh of relief we passed through the Strait of Hormuz and into the Persian Gulf. The only other notable event during our voyage through the Gulf was that Italian planes bombed the island of Bahrain. But according to eye witnesses they were flying so high that they didn't even hit the island, never mind the oil refineries which were obviously their targets.

As we reached the northern end of the Persian Gulf and were approaching Fao, the captain asked me to come up to his cabin. He told me that we were likely to run into trouble going up the Shat-el-Arab, which was the river formed by the confluence of the Tigris and Euphrates rivers, as the right bank was controlled by the Iranians and the left bank by the Iraqis. As the Iranians were what they called "belligerently neutral," they had threatened that if any of our ships crossed on to their side of the Shat-el-Arab they would open fire on us. The captain said that in case of emergency we should be prepared to defend the ship, and asked me to take suitable steps. So I agreed to do what I could.

At a subsequent conference with my officers and senior N.C.O.s we discussed the problem of what action to take in the event of such an emergency. As we had no sandbags we built small emplacements on the deck out of 80 lb bags of *atta* (the flour used by the Indian troops.) I then emphasised very strongly that no fire must be opened unless I gave specific orders, as we must at all costs avoid any action which would infringe the neutrality of Iran. I also stressed that only those men manning the emplacements would be allowed on deck once we had entered the Shat-el-Arab. All the Indian *sepoys* would be kept below decks to avoid any possible panic firing, which could have sparked off an international incident.

We then started to move slowly up the Shat-el-Arab keeping well to the Iraqi side. The river was pretty narrow and called for careful navigation to keep away from the Iranian bank. As we sailed along one could see that the Iranian side of the river bank was lined with armed troops looking very aggressive and definitely belligerent! However, we managed to negotiate the hundred and twenty miles of river without incident and arrived at Basra late in the afternoon.

Because the Iraqis were extremely hostile and their forces were in occupation of Basra, two Gurkha battalions were sent on in advance of the main body to make sure that our landing in Basra would not be interrupted. I gather that the Gurkhas landed without much opposition and the Iraqi forces then withdrew and set up camp a few miles from Shaiba. We learnt that most of the Iraqi officers had bolted into Iran, so that the force was commanded by N.C.Os. This fairly large and well-equipped force sitting in the desert was a constant menace, and after a short time a message was sent calling on them to surrender. They were given an ultimatum of twelve noon the next day to do so or be bombed.

Little did they know that to carry out this threat we only had two single-seater Audax planes. An adjustment was made to enable another person to sit behind the pilot, the idea being that an officer would sit holding a bomb in his arms.

The planes took off with instructions that they were not to drop their bombs until twelve noon. I gather that curiosity got the better of one of the young officers holding the bomb, and in craning his neck to look at the Iraqis the bomb slipped out of his clutches, fell and exploded. Luckily it didn't fall on the Iraqis, but close enough to give them a nasty fright, and within a short time a surrender party with white flag came into Shaiba. Subsequently they were all disarmed and I was surprised to see that their arms were more modern than ours. They had Bren guns which were quite new to us. Up to this point they had been equipped by Britain. A peace treaty was signed and they then became our "allies," although I never trusted the blighters! We then re-armed them and they carried out lines of communication duties.

22

Sand, flies and heat-stroke

Immediately after berthing an embarkation officer came on board and asked if I was the O.C. troops. He then told me that we must evacuate the ship within six hours.

"Six hours!" I said. "It'll take six days to unload this ship. We've got tents, rations for three months, ammunition and goodness knows what on board."

"Well, I'm sorry," he said, "but we need this ship as soon as possible to evacuate the thousands of refugees that are cluttering up the aerodrome. Your men can only take what they can carry ashore."

So we went ashore with as much as we could carry, and I was met by a young officer who had gone on ahead in a station wagon. He took me out to a place called Shaiba, a huge camp enclosed by barbed wire in the middle of the desert. We got there in the evening and the officer said: "I'm sorry, Sir, but I'm afraid we haven't got a tent for you."

"Of course not," I replied. "None of us has any tents, they're all in the ship. In any case, I wouldn't be happy sleeping in a tent if the men didn't have any."

So we just had to make the best of a bad job and doss down on the desert. I didn't realise at the time the danger of sleeping on the sand, but luckily I had a very portable camp bed about six inches off the ground on which I settled down as best I could.

At about four the next morning I was woken by one of my Indian officers who said: *Bahut bara tuckleif Sahib* (much trouble Sir.)

I went with him to where the men were sleeping and found that many of them had been bitten by scorpions during the night. The area was alive with these wretched pests, and you could see their holes everywhere. While we were wondering what on earth to do about them one of the Indian *sepoys* came forward and said that he could deal with the situation by means of an empty bottle. Somebody produced a bottle and in no time this chap had filled it full of scorpions. I asked him what he proposed to do with them and he said that he would cook them in boiling water, then strain the liquid and drink it. He told me that if I drank this liquid I would be as strong as a lion. I declined with thanks! Anyway, as we had insufficient bottles for this method we cleared most of the area by digging them out, and the next night we had far fewer casualties from scorpions.

The following day I went down to see the G.O.C. of the force, explained our conditions and asked him if he could give us some tents. He explained that there were no tents available and that we would just have to stick it out until they were able to fly some from India.

After about three days of living under these ghastly conditions with a temperature of one hundred and twenty-six degrees Fahrenheith in the shade — and there wasn't any shade — some tents arrived. Of course there were nothing like the number we wanted, and a tent that normally accommodated sixteen men had to take about forty. The situation eventually improved, but during this initial period we lost a lot of men from heatstroke and malaria.

Another big problem was food. The Iraqis were hostile and wouldn't sell us anything, so we lived on bully beef and dehydrated spuds, which turned black when you cooked them. We were also short of water to drink, and couldn't even restore our morale with a bit of booze. Fortunately there was a permanent R.A.F. station located near Shaiba so I went over to see the C.O. and asked if they could help us. He said he could let us have whisky at ten shillings a bottle and soda to go with it if we could provide the containers. This cheered us up a lot.

I then set about trying to improve the standard of the food in the messes. I told the mess secretary that I wanted to see all the mess servants. Eventually they were paraded and they looked like a gang of retired bandits. The first chap I came to was alleged to be the officers' mess cook. So I said to him: "What experience have you had in cooking?"

"Oh, Sahib!" he said, "I'm not a cook — I'm a carpenter."

"Well, how on earth did you get this job?" I asked him.

He replied: "When they were recruiting at Poona the officer asked me if I could cook. I told him I couldn't, but he said 'Well from now on you're a cook — Class 1'."

So that was the type of servant we got in the mess. I went along to the sergeants' mess to find out how they were getting on, and their conditions were even worse than ours, so it was obvious that something had to be done, and quickly.

I had all the N.C.Os paraded and asked if any of them knew anything about cooking. Three or four chaps stepped forward, and one of them said he'd been a chef at one of the London hotels. So I told him he'd better take over the job of running the officers' mess, and one of the others was detailed to take over the sergeants' mess.

Of course at that stage there was very little to cook, but things did improve when the Iraqis changed their attitude and started to sell us lamb, eggs and vegetables. The eggs were hard-boiled to prevent them from going bad.

Bathing was also a bugbear. Although we were camped practically on the bank of the Euphrates river bathing was strictly prohibited owing to the prevalence of bilharzia, a most painful and at that time a practically incurable disease. I used to manage a bath of sorts about once in three days. One of the few things that was in abundant supply was petrol, so we used to wash our clothes in it!

The river banks were lined with date palms, dates being one of the chief exports of Iraq. As the dates ripened they attracted billions of little eye flies which then invaded the camp, so that we had to wear nets over our faces when having meals. Malarial mosquitoes and millions of house flies were additional pests, and deaths from malaria assumed rather frightening proportions. Everyone suffered from prickly heat and mine went septic so that I could hardly bear to wear my battledress.

Every morning just as the sun came up a slight breeze would blow, and this would lift the very fine dust off the desert to an altitude of about four hundred feet, and conditions became rather like a London fog. Visibility was reduced to practically nil. As our tents were widely dispersed against the possibility of enemy air attack it became very difficult to find one's way from tent to tent without getting lost. To overcome this problem we had to peg down tapes between the tents indicating the direction. I learnt this trick during World War I. These conditions usually persisted all day until the wind dropped in the evening, and with it the cloud of sand.

To give some idea of the intensity of this dust cloud: After the Iraqis surrendered, some bankers were flown out from India to take over the enemy banks. They landed at Shaiba and then flew on to Baghdad, intending to return that evening. The dust cloud conditions prevailed and on their return we could hear the plane going round and round looking for a chance to land. Eventually the noise of the engine ceased and we presumed that they had landed. However, it was discovered next morning that it had crashed in the desert and that all the occupants were dead. I hope that they were killed in the crash, as their bodies were found in the plane and had been mutilated by jackals.

The Iraqis had destroyed the railway line between Basra and Baghdad by flooding it, so communications between the two were impossible except by air. The R.A.F. station at Habanir near Baghdad was surrounded by Iraqi troops, which prevented the aerodrome from being used. In order to relieve this position a squadron of Blenheim bombers was flown from North Africa to Shaiba. These used to carry out daily bombing raids on the Iraqi positions round Baghdad. One evening we heard the usual noise of planes, when suddenly there was a series of deafening explosions quite close to our camp. I presumed that we were being bombed by the enemy, as we had been warned of this possibility. I was lying in bed in my tent and when the "bombing" started, I rolled out of bed and into a slit trench in the tent which had been prepared for such an emergency. My orderly, who normally slept outside, rolled in on top of me. The "bombing" ceased and I walked across to the aerodrome to discover that it was one of our own Blenheims which had hit the barbed wire surrounding the camp on take-off, causing all the bombs to explode. Needless to say the crew all perished.

Guarding our aerodrome at this time was a regiment of Iraqi Levies specially enlisted for the job. They were tall, fine-looking chaps, but they had no guts at all. As soon as this bombing, as they thought, began, most of these Iraqi chaps started legging it as fast as they could in the general direction of Fao. I got talking to the chap commanding the Iraq Levies, a British captain. He told me they had just had a roll call and out of about nine hundred men less than two hundred had answered the roll. I asked him if he thought they would return, and he said he thought it was extremely unlikely.

So we took over their barracks; one for the officers' mess, one for the sergeants' mess and the rest were divided between the men. They were extraordinary places, built of brick and dug right down into the ground with only the roof showing. This provided us with cool accommodation by day, but were very hot at night, so we normally slept in the open.

My unit was widely dispersed on account of possible enemy bombing, and I used a station wagon when going to inspect it. One morning I had driven out about three miles into the desert when I remembered something I should have done before leaving H.Q. Fortunately a Royal Corps of Signals station was nearby. This consisted of a caravan with a 'paulin extension, under which a British Tommy was sitting at a table. I drove up as near as I could and shouted to him not to come out, but that I would give him the message from the car. However, despite this he rose and came towards me, saluted, and promptly fell back onto the ground unconscious. My orderly and I picked him up, put him in the back of the station wagon and told the N.C.O. in charge that I was taking him back to Shaiba. The first hospital that we came to was an Indian Field Hospital where I happened to know the C.O., a jolly good chap. I left this poor fellow in charge of the authorities saying that I would come back later that day to see how he was. I then carried on with my inspection work.

I returned to the hospital at about half past six in the evening, went into the C.O.'s office and asked: "Well, how's my young friend that I left here this morning?"

"Oh!" he said, "I'm sorry but we buried him about an hour ago. He didn't recover from the heatstroke. We did everything possible but he never regained consciousness and then died."

Heatstroke was one of our worst enemies in Iraq. The patient developed a very high temperature, the internal organs ceased to function and unless the body temperature could be reduced quickly the person died. The treatment was to put the patient in a bath of ice.

We weren't doing any actual fighting at this time and the death of this young fellow and many others seemed such an appalling waste of life.

Travelling from Shaiba to Basra there was only one track through the desert, and if you got off it by any chance you were literally bogged down. This was caused by seepage from the rivers and because of this condition orders were issued that sand mats must be carried at all times. These were placed under the wheels of the vehicles enabling the tyres to get a grip.

One morning when I was driving into Basra I noticed a car, surrounded by staff officers, which appeared to be in trouble some distance from the road. I stopped my car and walked towards them rather cautiously because of the bog-like condition of the sand. As I reached the car I could see that the officers were all high ranking chaps covered with red tabs, and among them I noticed Bill Slim. He was by now a general and had recently been appointed G.O.C. PAI Force. I went up to him, saluted and said: "Are you in trouble Sir?"

"Yes, we jolly well are," he replied. Then, recognising me, he said: "Hello Hodgson, we meet again."

"Yes Sir," I said, "and under rather unfortunate circumstances."

"Yes!" he said. "If these bloody people who drive cars would obey my orders and carry sand mats we wouldn't be in this trouble. I bet you've got yours Hodgson."

"Yes Sir," I replied, feeling rather smug. "You can have them."

So I shouted to my orderly and he came across carrying four sand mats and we soon had the G.O.C. and his staff back on the road again.

After the Iraqis had capitulated and been disarmed the situation became reasonably quiet. I was ordered to do a "recce" in the vicinity of the Hammar Lake. It was a large shallow lake about five miles from Shaiba. I went out by car with a couple of brother officers and drove as near as we could to the lake. Looking through my field glasses the whole surface seemed to be covered with a white fluffy substance. We couldn't make out what it was, so I pulled out my revolver and fired a shot in the air, whereupon the entire surface of the lake rose up about fifty feet. It turned out to be hundreds of flamingoes, and what a superb sight they were, with their beautiful pink and white colouring. They hovered motionless for a few minutes and then sank gracefully back onto the lake.

We then pushed on to have a look at Kut-el-Amara, the scene of a very grim battle and siege between the British and Turkish forces in World War I. The fortifications were still more or less intact. The British forces suffered enormous casualties there from dysentery, enteric and typhoid.

On another occasion I was driving slowly across the desert when some distance away the whole surface seemed to be moving. On closer inspection I saw that it was birds, which turned out to be imperial sand grouse. They were lovely looking creatures, added to which I knew they were damn good eating. So I dashed back to the mess and found several fellows sitting there. I asked if any of them had done any shooting with shot guns and they said they had. We managed to collect about a dozen guns and some ammunition, made a plan of action and in several cars started out for the area where I had spotted the sand grouse. I explained to them that wasn't a sporting event, but a means of getting some fresh meat for the pot, even if it meant browning them on the ground. So we circled round the birds and at the appropriate moment I opened up and the others followed suit. Between us we managed to get about seventy sand grouse, and the officers and N.O.Cs had the best meal since arriving in Iraq. We realised that it was very unsporting, but it was a case of "needs must . . ."

I was lying in my bed one night when to my amazement I heard rain for the first time since coming to Iraq. I stripped to the buff and stood outside my tent with the rain teeming down onto me and my septic prickly heat. What absolute bliss it was.

Three or four days after this deluge the whole desert burst into a blaze of colour. This was due to thousands of little crocuses which had been lying dormant suddenly coming into bloom. It was a wonderful sight after the monotony of endless, lifeless sand — or as the British Tommy described it in a letter home — "miles and miles of bugger all!" However, as we had no more rain the floral display gradually faded and died.

A rather amusing incident occurred while we were at Shaiba in connection with the cooking of the Indian troops' food. We had been using a sort of miniature flame thrower for all our cooking requirements. Then one of my Indian officers asked if we could get some firewood for the Indian troops to cook with, as they would find it more suitable. I told him that I was going to Basra and if he came with me we would see what we could find.

On going through the outskirts of Basra I noticed a sweet factory that specialised in making liquorice sweets, and in the yard I saw a huge pile of timber. We drove into the yard and met the proprietor (a Baghdadi Jew) who showed us round the factory and gave us masses of sweets for the troops. He was so friendly that I felt rather embarrassed that I had every intention of taking his pile of timber.

On leaving the factory I said: "I'm afraid I'm going to commandeer that heap of wood."

"What wood?" he asked.

"That pile you've got out in the yard," I replied.

"Wood?" he said. "That's not wood, that's raw liquorice!"

My Indian officer and I hurriedly left the factory feeling complete fools.

23

General Bill Slim

My time in Iraq was showing signs of petering out. The conditions under which we had been living brought about a recurrence of my old complaint, amoebic dysentery. I was put into Margill hospital where I underwent some pretty filthy treatment which wasn't successful and it was decided to fly me back to Bombay. In the end, however, they couldn't get me onto a plane so I went by sea in a hospital ship. On arrival in Bombay I was put back into hospital at Colaba where I spent three weeks, and was then declared fit for service. My wife, who had been living in Poona all this time, was able to join me in Bombay. On leaving hospital I was posted to Chaklala near Rawalpindi where I was made O.C. of the station. My immediate command was the huge ordnance depot there.

One weekend, while visiting Murree on leave, we were staying at Flashman's Hotel. Walking into the foyer I was surprised to see General Claude Auchinleck sitting there alone. Having met "The Auk," the name by which he was generally known in India, on a previous occasion, I saluted and greeted him. Although I had heard rumours about what had happened I pretended not to know.

"What are you doing here Sir?" I asked.

"I wish I knew," he replied, and went on to say that he had no idea what his future would be. It could even be a bowler hat.

Apparently the Auk had been relieved of his command as

Commander-in-Chief Middle East by Winston Churchill, in favour of General Alexander. Most people felt it was unjustified as he was held in high regard in India.

However, we were all very pleased when in June 1943 the Auk was appointed Commander-in-Chief India, succeeding General Wavell who then became Viceroy. His appointment was extremely popular with officers and men alike, and he was considered to be a very fine soldier. The next time I met him was at Quetta in Baluchistan.

This job lasted about six months. In the summer of 1942 I was posted to join the H.Q. of the 15th Indian Corps forming in Calcutta. Wives were not permitted as this was a war zone so once again we were separated.

On the way down to Calcutta by train we stopped at a small wayside station, and I got out to stretch my legs. On walking down to the end of the platform I noticed a staff officer covered with "red tabs" and as I drew closer I saw that it was my old friend Bill Slim. I went up to him, saluted and greeted him.

"Hello, Hodgson," he said. "We meet once again. Where are you going this time?"

"I've been posted to H.Q. of a comic outfit known as the 15th Indian Mobile Corps forming in Calcutta,"I said. "Have you ever known anything that's mobile in India? I wonder who's commanding it?"

In a quiet voice he replied: "I am."

I apologised for my remark and he said: "That's all right, Hodgson. Come into my carriage and we'll travel the rest of the journey together."

So General Slim and I eventually arrived in Calcutta where it was hot, humid and sticky. The city was in a tense state. The Japs had landed in Burma and pushed the Burma Corps right up to the north of the country. They were in full retreat, and were naturally a pretty demoralised force. General Slim had been in command of the Burma Corps and was now in the process of forming the 15th Indian Corps with the object of re-invading Burma.

We were billeted in private houses at Barrackpore on the outskirts of Calcutta and the Corps doctor and I shared a room in a private house belonging to the manager of the Titaghur Paper Mills. He was a bit browned off at having officers billeted with him, although he did benefit by our sharing our rations with him. Food at that time was pretty short in Calcutta. Troops were pouring into the place, mostly British units completely unused to the Indian climate. The monsoon was in full swing and the poor devils were in tents living under the most appalling and unhealthy conditions.

The Japs didn't worry us to any great extent as they were fully occupied chasing the Burma Corps. They did, however, harass us on the Sundarbans, which is a jungly, marshy delta formed by the Ganges and Hooghly rivers. They used to come over in small boats from Chittagong in Burma, making sorties by day and night. Trying to shoot them with rifles was well nigh impossible, owing to the thickness of the jungle, so it was decided to try and deal with them by means of twelve bore shotguns. To this end Bill Slim asked me to go into Calcutta and commandeer as many such guns as I could. There was one very high-class gun shop, so I went and asked if they had any stock. They didn't have many, so I had to commandeer some of the guns they were holding for private customers who had left them for safe-keeping on account of the war. I also took all the ammunition they had in stock.

As I was driving away from the gun shop a Jap plane flew over dropping anti-personnel bombs. One of them dropped at the entrance to the shop I had just left, blowing in the door and killing and wounding several British troops standing on the corner. The result of this light bombing was that half the Indians living in Calcutta bolted back onto the mainland.

Of course, Calcutta was a huge city with many millions of inhabitants. It was connected to the mainland by a pontoon bridge and a huge new bridge which had just been completed. If the Japs invaded Calcutta, which we expected them to do at any moment, the plan was to blow up these bridges once our troops had withdrawn to the mainland. As we had no hope of holding the Japs at that time the idea was to carry out a "scorched earth" policy.

Another problem was that, should we have to withdraw, the

civilian population would certainly block the roads in their efforts to get out of Calcutta. To minimise this every bicycle in the city was confiscated and placed in Calcutta Fort. Another reason for doing this was to prevent them falling into Japanese hands, as they were known to use them for patrols to harass retreating forces. To further prevent congestion on the roads all bullock carts were to be "grounded" in the event of invasion by removing their wheels. As it so happened the Japs never attempted a landing so the magnificent new Howrah Bridge was saved.

During this time the Burma Corps was still being pursued by the Japs and had reached a place called Imphal, from where they were going to be evacuated into India. Bill Slim sent for me one day and said that the remnants of the Burma Corps were coming into India and that we were going to send up a train-load of food, drink and clothing to welcome them on arrival.

He asked me to go down to Howrah Station and requisition the Shillong mail train in order to deliver the stuff to the troops. When I got to the station the train was actually standing at the platform.

I went into the station-master's office and said: "I want to commandeer several carriages on that mail train, and if necessary, the whole train."

"Oh!" he said. "You can't do that, the train's fully booked," and was most unco-operative.

I then told him the reason why I was doing this, and that our troops were coming out of Burma. His whole attitude changed immediately.

"You can have as many trains as you like," he said. "My boy is coming out with that lot."

So they cleared several carriages, we loaded our goods into them and off the train went.

I was to meet this station-master on another occasion. We had a telephone call from him one day to say that someone had put a bomb in his office and could we come down and dispose of it. Well, as I was supposed to be a ballistic expert I was sent down to the station with one of my warrant officers to deal with the situation. They had placed the alleged bomb in a bucket of water and were giving it a very wide berth. I found that it was a Mills grenade which was perfectly harmless as the pin was still in position. I threw it up in the air a couple of times to prove the point, but the station-master and his staff ran like shot rabbits. It had apparently been found under a seat in one of the carriages. I took it away and destroyed it.

To capture a Japanese prisoner was almost impossible, as whenever they were in danger of being captured they committed "Hari-kiri." This was done by means of a grenade which they carried. They would remove the pin, press it to their tummies and would be killed by the explosion. To a Japanese soldier it was considered a disgrace to be captured alive. This was all connected with the Japanese code of chivalry called *bushido*.

An extraordinary example of this occurred near a place called Imphal. It was one of the last attempts made by the Japs to get into India. They launched a very strong attack which nearly succeeded against a position held by a British and Indian battalion. They made two more attacks which also failed and then appeared to withdraw altogether. Patrols eventually made contact some fifteen miles away where they found the remains of the Jap force all dead, having committed hari-kiri. They were in a very emaciated condition having had very little food during their advance through Burma, which probably contributed to their suicidal action.

While we were still in Calcutta the Japs frequently sent planes over on reconnaissance. On one occasion the plane developed engine trouble and crash-landed. The pilot was found alive but unconscious. He was the first prisoner we'd managed to capture alive. He eventually regained consciousness and wouldn't give us any information, which he was perfectly justified in withholding as a prisoner of war. He remained silent for three days, and of course under the Geneva Convention we were not permitted to force him to talk.

Well, after about three days he suddenly spoke, and said: "All right, now I speak. I will tell you anything that I know."

He explained his change of attitude by saying that as he had been captured alive he would not be accepted by his country and would never be able to return there.

After about three months in Calcutta and Barrackpore it was decided that we should move up to Ranchi in the Bihar province, some two hundred miles away. The Eastern Army H.Q., under General Irwin, would then move into our old H.Q. at Barrackpore. It was from there that General Irwin launched his disastrous Arakan campaign.

Ranchi, being a semi-hill station, had a much more equable climate than the steamy heat of Calcutta, and with its wide variety of terrain, including jungles, rivers and open country, it provided an ideal training area for the troops who were destined to reinvade Burma. Most of the staff, myself included, were given quarters in the station hotel, while Bill Slim and his senior officers were located in the summer residence of the Governor of Bengal.

We used to have conferences every day, and very often after the conference Bill Slim would drop into my office for a friendly talk. He and I got on very well and he was a marvellous man to work with — he was so unassuming and never pushed his rank. To give an idea of the type of fellow he was: He told us one morning at conference that he had been walking down the main street of Ranchi and that he had passed a number of British troops who failed to salute him. They were men from a division that had had a bad mauling in North Africa and their morale was very low. As a result they had become rather bolshy. Bill Slim's method of dealing with this situation was to salute the men himself as he passed them. In no time at all, shame-faced British troops were saluting him as they were supposed to do. This was a far more tactful and effective method of dealing with the situation than taking disciplinary action, and was typical of the man.

One day Bill Slim came into my office and said: "Hodgson, you're in real trouble!"

So I said "Why Sir?"

"Well," he said, "apparently there's been a complete muck-up over the forming of the support and recce divisions which the commander-in-chief is so anxious should go into Burma before the monsoon breaks. All their equipment has been sent to the wrong place and there's not sufficient time to readjust it before the monsoon comes and makes it impossible to move anything. Therefore we won't be able to carry out this operation and you have been blamed for muddling it."

I was absolutely stunned by this statement and replied: "Well Sir, I know absolutely nothing about it, although I had heard off the record that these divisions were forming. I have never been consulted and I have received no orders of any kind."

"I believe you Hodgson," he replied, "but it's all very extraordinary, and the situation is so serious that the commander-in-chief himself (who at that time was General Archibald Wavell) is coming down to see you personally and to hear your explanation. He'll be here tomorrow."

I replied: "Well Sir, I can only tell him what I've told you."

"Right," he said. "Tomorrow morning when the commander-in-chief comes you'll be sent for. Just go up to him and he'll hear what you've got to say. He probably won't make any comment, but don't overdo it, just say what you've got to say and then beat it."

I had known Archie Wavell some years before in Abbottabad and I remembered that he had a mannerism when conducting an interview. He had one blind eye and when he wanted to terminate the interview he would turn his head so that his dud eye was facing you. This was your *congé.*

The next morning came and I went up to the commander-in-chief and he said. "Hullo, you're Hodgson aren't you?"

"Yes Sir," I replied.

"Now tell me what you know about this affair," he said. So I told him exactly what I had told Bill Slim, that I knew nothing at all about it.

"Is that all?" Archie Wavell asked.

"Yes Sir!" I replied, and fell out.

It was subsequently discovered that our people at army headquarters in Simla had bungled the placing of equipment and were looking for a scapegoat. They picked me for this job and that was their second blunder! However, their plan didn't work, and when Archie Wavell returned to army headquarters a couple of our chaps were sacked, and I wasn't a bit sorry for the blighters.

On one occasion when Bill Slim was talking to me he mentioned the fact that it would be about three months before we would be in a position to go back into Burma. He then said that he thought it would be a good idea to let the married officers have their wives with them in Ranchi, and asked me if I would like my wife to join me. I naturally replied that I would be delighted. General Slim then said that the condition was that she would have to do war-work while in Ranchi. As she was already knee-deep in it this presented no problem.

I managed to make contact with my wife by telegram and sub-sequently by phone. She at that time was living at a place called Murree in the Punjab hills. We arranged that if she could get to Delhi by train I would meet her there.

I realised that it was likely to be a pretty hazardous journey as Gandhi and his gang were very active at that time. There was a lot of wrecking, burning and derailing of trains, and a number of British officers had already been murdered by Gandhi's followers in the so-called passive resistance movement. The Congress Party in Orissa, Bengal and Bihar were doing all they could to impede our war effort, under the misguided idea that the Japs, if they got into India, would hand over power to the Congress Party. We eventually managed to get the situation under control by arresting Gandhi and many of his followers.

My wife, who was never lacking courage in adversity, agreed to make the journey to Delhi and said she would leave the following day. I left Ranchi the next day as well and we eventually met up in Delhi. She had had a most frightening trip. Trains had been derailed and burnt, and it took her two days to do an eight-hour journey. We spent a couple of days in Delhi and then prepared for the return trip to Calcutta. I filled a large ice-box with food and drink, and it was just as well I did. The journey down to Calcutta was absolute hell. The whole place was in a turmoil, with troops all over the place guarding stations, bridges, and other installations, and one expected the line to be blown up at any minute. The trains were running in convoys, two or three trains travelling together with armed guards on each one. Needless to say there was no food or drink, so the ice-box and its contents were a godsend. In spite of all this it was lovely to be with my wife again after all our long separations.

We reached Calcutta, spent a night at the Bengal Club and then went on to Ranchi by train. My wife started on her war work in places like hospitals and canteens, and I got on with the training programme so that we would be completely mobile when the necessity arose.

On Christmas Eve, 1942, my wife and I were just about to leave to spend Christmas in Calcutta in one of the hotels, when I happened to switch on the radio and heard that at that very moment Calcutta was being bombed by the Japs. We decided that Ranchi would be a more peaceful place to spend Christmas and gave Calcutta a miss.

Fresh units kept arriving to join our corps and we reached a standard to the satisfaction of our corps commander, no mean achievement. Even our Indian clerks were rendered mobile so that they could take part in the fighting if necessary. No-one was exempt from square bashing, rifle practice, and similar training.

Shortly after we moved up to Ranchi from Calcutta, two rather depleted Chinese divisions were evacuated by air from north-east Burma. They were the remnants of General Stilwell's command — an American general known as "Vinegary Joe." They had been completely cut off and were in a very poor physical condition. The American Air Force carried out the evacuation very successfully, and landed them at Ranchi. The Chinese troops destroyed and left practically all their arms and equipment in Burma so that the planes could carry more men.

After a period of rest we re-equipped and re-armed them, and they were also provided with mountain artillery — 3.7" Howitzers. They were very enthusiastic about handling their new equipment, and their two Chinese generals were even more so. They had pronounced American accents. These two were like a couple of schoolboys trying out their new "toys," and were most intrigued with our "flame thrower" type of cooking equipment. As far as I remember the Chinese eventually went back into Burma with General Wingate and the Chindits.

However, before we were ordered to go back into Burma my personal part in the show came to an end. Fate, in the shape of a recurrence of amoebic dysentery, put me out of action and back into hospital. Subsequently I was given a medical board hearing, and they decided that my service in India should be terminated and that I should return to the U.K. Of course this was totally impractical as I was Indian Army, and to be sent back to England would be tantamount to getting a bowler hat. I pointed this out to the president of the medical board and he again emphasised the seriousness of my condition, and that to stay on in India was likely to bring about my demise. However, he said that if I could get posted to a hill station with a colder climate he would agree to this.

So I told the powers that be in Simla that if they wanted to get rid of me this was an ideal opportunity, but otherwise they would have to send me to a more suitable climate.

It was heartbreaking to have to leave the Corps, and particularly Bill Slim at this stage of the campaign, but it was inevitable. I should have liked to have been able to follow the campaign to finality and accompany Bill Slim when he turned "Defeat into Victory," to quote the title of his own book. Such men as he are not often met.

24

I'm soldiering no more

They posted me to Quetta in Baluchistan, as chief ordnance officer. It was a long train journey, right across northern India and then south west towards Karachi, and we were thankful to arrive and install ourselves in the very comfortable Chiltan Hotel, named after one of the high mountains in the district.

Quetta was about six thousand feet above sea level. It had a hot, dry summer, but the father and mother of a winter with temperatures dropping to ten degrees below freezing, and a killer of a wind known as the Khojak, which blew down from the Khojak Pass. This wind, plus the freezing temperatures, caused the death of many Baluchis, despite their sheepskin-lined boots and jackets. We used warm sheets on our bed in winter and had to buy special clothing: Woollen vests, flannel shirts, woollen battledress, topped by a British Warm and gloves were the regular form of dress. The icicles hanging from the eaves of our quarters were so thick that you couldn't reach round them with both arms.

Quetta was notorious for earthquakes. Every day there would be a 'quake of some kind, varying in intensity from a mild tremor to a severe 'quake. The cantonment was almost entirely rebuilt after the devastating earthquake of 1935. Representatives were sent from India to Japan to study the method of anti-earthquake building, and as a result the whole of Quetta was rebuilt on these lines. The houses were constructed with regard to the contours of the earth's surface, and I gathered that fairly big buildings were built on the same principle as a ship — in two sections.

My particular assignment was to plan and rebuild the ordnance depot so that all the buildings were earthquake-proof. Incidentally, the British government were footing a bill of some six million pounds for this job.

The office block was very modern, even to the extent of providing indoor sanitation for the Indian clerks. Initially this proved to be a disaster as far as the Hindus were concerned, as they used smooth stones instead of toilet paper and succeeded in blocking the whole sewerage system! So we had to re-educate them in the correct usage.

At the same time I had to build an underground ammunition depot which had to be air-conditioned. It was specifically for the storage of anti-aircraft ammunition as the Germans were in a position to carry out an air attack for which we would get the maximum of a few minutes' warning. As this whole project was very expensive the British government sent out a representative in the form of a general to inspect the whole place. At that time Baluchistan came under direct British control.

When I showed this general round the depot and ammunition store, of which I was rather proud, he told me he thought we had been unnecessarily extravagant with regard to the air-conditioning. However, I pointed out that with the extremes of temperature from which Quetta suffered, from a hundred degrees in summer down to minus ten degrees Fahrenheit in winter, it was absolutely necessary if we were to keep the ammunition for any length of time. It was essential to store it in a dry and even temperature all year round. I think I succeeded in convincing him, but I don't think he knew very much about ammunition storage and was really only concerned with the expense.

Some time in 1944 a directive was issued to all commanding officers in India to start breeding — with immediate effect! However, before I had a chance to discuss this rather disturbing order with my wife, I read the rest of the directive and found to my great relief that the authorities were referring to the production of food and not to the propagation of army personnel!

At that time in India we were beginning to suffer from a mild shortage of food, such as meat, poultry, eggs and bacon, the type of food favoured by Europeans. As a result of the war the European population in terms of troops had increased tremendously, and more food had to be produced, as very little could be imported.

I had a conference with my officers and we decided to launch the campaign by breeding chickens. I knew little or nothing about chickens and my British officers were just as ignorant. However, one of my Indian officers had some knowledge, so we sent him off to buy the necessary breeding stock. He had to go to Meerut, near Delhi, where the army had a breeding depot in order to get really first-class birds with which to start our "farm." This was a return journey of some two thousand miles. There was no nearer place of supply at that time and, being poor specimens, the local hens were quite useless for our purpose.

I gave the officer what I thought was ample money and off he went to Meerut. On arrival there he wired me to say that he hadn't sufficient money to buy the pedigree chickens we were after. I wired him back some more cash and eventually he arrived back with his precious cargo of some fifty birds, fully grown White Leghorns and Rhode Island Red hens, plus a couple of cockerels.

For the price he'd paid for these birds I felt they ought to lay golden eggs, but my Indian officer said that they were well worth the money as they were an excellent combination. The White Leghorns were prolific layers and the Rhode Islands were good table birds.

So we set about converting barracks to accommodate these aristocrats of the poultry world, and training *sepoys* to look after them. Jenny, the wife of one of my officers, offered to supervise the running of the chicken farm.

The White Leghorns were soon in full production, and as the eggs mounted up we started to think about hatching them. We hadn't enough broody hens, so we built some incubators for the job, each one capable of taking about two hundred and fifty eggs. In the end we had six hundred eggs all ready to be incubated. As the period of incubation came to an end the excitement became intense.

One day I was talking to the general and he asked me how we were getting on with the farming business.

"Well," I said, "we're doing our best. I'd like you to come over one day and attend a mass birth. We're expecting at least five hundred little ones."

"Oh!" he said. "Are you?"

The day of the expected hatching arrived and Jenny informed me that the chickens could start hatching at any moment. So I phoned the general and said that if he came round at three o'clock that afternoon he'd see something.

Well, sure enough the general arrived with his A.D.C. and we all stood around the incubators waiting for something to happen. After about an hour not a single ruddy chicken had appeared and the general was champing at the bit.

"I can't wait any longer," he barked. "I never thought you'd get anything out of those bloody boxes anyway," and he and his entourage stomped out of the maternity ward.

Of course I felt a complete fool and so did all concerned. Jenny was rushing about like a broody hen and could offer no explanation to my question of: "What the devil's happened?"

"I don't know," she wailed, by now almost in tears.

I went over to one of the incubators and took out an egg and broke it open. Inside was a fully formed little chick — dead. I went to another incubator and took out another egg. The same result. All the chickens were dead. It was then discovered that Jenny, in order to expedite the hatching process, probably in view of the General's visit, had turned up the heat of the incubators and in so doing had roasted the poor little devils alive.

I was very fed up about the whole thing and decided to take over the incubating part of the farm myself, with the help of some *sepoys* whom I trained. I was determined to make a success of the venture and prove to the general that we weren't such complete half-wits as we appeared.

So we built up another stock of eggs and repeated the whole operation again. On the appointed day I rang the old general and asked if he could bring himself to give us another chance and come down and have a look-see.

The old boy duly arrived and witnessed the hatching of some five hundred and fifty little chicks. Once hatched the chicks were put into brooders.

Flushed with success we decided to expand our poultry activities and launched out on ducks. We converted another barrackroom which had access to a huge fire tank which was filled with water to provide a "pond." The ducks flourished, but there was no sign of any eggs. Mystified, we eventually consulted headquarters at Simla and an expert was sent down.

"What time do you let them out in the morning?" the expert asked the *sepoy* who looked after them. He replied that it was about 6 a.m.

"Oh! That's far too early," he said. "They haven't had a chance to lay. Never let them out before 9 a.m."

So we took his advice and sure enough there were eggs galore the next morning. It then occurred to me that the ducks must have been laying somewhere all this time, so I had the pond drained. There were eggs all over the bottom. We collected them, cooked them and fed them to the chickens as protein.

We put the first twelve duck eggs into the incubator, and managed to hatch twelve little ducklings. My wife took a great interest in them and christened them the Twelve Twerps.

From ducks we went on to turkeys. We went in for a breed called Hollands. They grew to an enormous size and were very handsome birds. Although supposedly difficult to rear we had great success with ours and they were much in demand at Christmas time.

Our next project was rabbits. We prepared a concrete-lined pit for them which we filled with earth and surrounded with wire netting to prevent them burrowing out or escaping. We put the rabbits in this place and they seemed to be quite happy, but after about a week they had all disappeared. They had burrowed down into the earth and only seemed to appear at night. So if we wanted to get a rabbit we had to shoot them after dark.

The farm went from strength to strength and we repaid the loan we had borrowed from the government and still had a handsome credit. We used to sell the produce to local army units and also to Baluchi farmers. We let the latter have them at a reduced rate in order to improve their own stock, as the local chicken was a miserable creature.

It wasn't all plain sailing. At one point we had an outbreak of Newcastle disease, much dreaded among poultry farmers. Once again our expert from Simla came down. The diseased birds had to be killed and the healthy ones were all innoculated.

My posting to Quetta lasted until the end of the war, by which time the huge ordnance depot had been completed and had been in use for some time.

With the end of the war came the offer of promotion to brigadier with a posting to a new station in the Central Province of India. This was subject to my being passed fit by the medical authorities in Quetta. I knew the staff surgeon quite well, and showed him the letter, saying that I presumed there would be no problem as I had been in much better health since coming to Quetta. To my surprise he said: "I'll have to take you into hospital for a complete check-up."

After ten days of tests in hospital he said: "I'm sorry, but I can't pass you fit for that job."

My wife was not in very good health, and as I was of pensionable age we decided to retire and go and live in the U.K. So I tendered my resignation and was given twelve months leave on full pay pending retirement.

Prior to our leaving Quetta the Commander-in-Chief, Field Marshal Sir Claude Auchinleck, came to Quetta to inspect all units, and spent nearly a week with mine. On completion of his inspection he complimented me on the standard of the unit saying: "Damn good show, Hodgson. It's chaps like you that we need to rebuild the Indian Army to its pre-war standard."

I asked him how long he thought the present regime in India would last. He replied that he thought at least ten years. I didn't mention the fact that I was proposing to retire, but I was very glad that I had done so because, within a year of my leaving India, the whole set-up had blown up and India had become independent.

However, I did miss the "golden handshake" to the extent of several thousand pounds.

So it was that in March 1946 I took leave of my unit and the country and its people which I had learned to love, and where I had spent twenty-five extremely happy years. After many farewell parties and presentations we were heavily garlanded and boarded the train for Karachi. There we embarked on the British India Line ship S.S. Karanja due to sail via the African East Coast ports to Durban, South Africa. Having never been via the Cape route we thought it would be interesting to see something of Africa through its ports, and as we had all the time in the world it would be a change from the Mediterranean route.

The voyage was most enjoyable and we called at the Seychelles, Mombasa, Dar-es-Salaam, Zanzibar and Lourenco Marques — or Maputo, as it's now called.

When we got to Durban we were met by the embarkation officer as I was still on the active list although pending retirement. He told me that there was no likelihood of an onward passage for some weeks. So we put up at an hotel to await developments.

While I was in Simla, just prior to leaving India, I had picked up a magazine in the library which was produced by the 1820 Settlers Association. I noticed that they had an office in Durban.

The Association was formed in 1920 to commemmorate the centenary of the landing of British settlers in 1820, and to assist settlers in this century to come to South Africa. The original settlers consisted of 4 000 courageous people — men, women and children — who were selected from 92 000 applicants. They came from all walks of life at a time when Britain was suffering from the effects of the Napoleonic Wars. The scheme was aided by the British Government to the tune of fifty-thousand pounds sterling, and twenty-one small ships transported them to Algoa Bay, later to become Port Elizabeth.

The scheme was instigated by the then Governor of the Cape Colony, Lord Charles Somerset, in order to populate the Eastern Cape and to provide a buffer against the African tribes to the North. He painted a word picture of a land with fertile soil, healthy climate and every possibility of prosperity, but failed to mention the total lack of housing, schools, hospitals or any of the comforts of a civilised society. These intrepid settlers somehow managed to survive through grit and tenacity, and it was these people that the Association was formed to honour — a hundred years later.

A London office was established where settlers were first interviewed, and branches were opened throughout South Africa. At the time of writing half-a-million settlers have been helped by the Association.

As I was at a loose end while waiting for a passage I looked up the 1820 Settlers Association and they asked me to join their committee. By the time we were offered passages to England some eighteen months later I had become secretary of the Durban branch and had decided to become a settler in South Africa myself.

I remained branch secretary of the Association for eighteen years, during which time I interviewed and tried to help some fifty-thousand people. They were mainly from Britain, but many came from India, the Far East and Kenya.

So instead of the leisurely retirement I had anticipated I found myself working far harder than I had ever done in the army, but it was a satisfying and rewarding job. At one time I was interviewing settlers at the rate of one thousand a month, and having to find accommodation and employment for all of them, quite apart from sorting out their personal and matrimonial problems.

But that's another story!

INDEX

Frazer, Maj. Gen. W.A.K. 170
French 17, 20, 25-7, 34

G
Gandhi 190
Ganges river 185
Gas attacks 17, 18, 27-9
Geddes Commission 111
Geneva Convention 58
George, Lloyd 65
Germans 2-4, 7, 10, 11, 17, 18, 21, 22, 25-9, 34, 35, 37-40, 170-2, 194
Ghats 114, 165, 167
Gneisenau (ship) 164
Godavari river 116-7
Grand Trunk Road 105
Gulf of Oman 172
Gurkhas 86, 95-7, 99, 123, 145, 152, 154-5, 173
Gwalior, Maharajah of 120, 122, 126

H
Habanir 178
Haig, General Sir Douglas 35
Hammar lake 181
Harfleur 45
Harmuz, strait of 172
Hill 60, 18
Himalayas 95-6, 123, 132-3, 140, 155
Hindu Kush 155
Hitler 163
Hodgson (2nd/lt.) (later, Colonel) Clarence:
Volunteers, World War I page 1
Serves in France & Belgium 1-41
Posted to Ireland 41
Marries 42
Trains as riding instructor 47
Posted to Norwich 53
Posted to Dublin 56
Posted to Northern Ireland 57
Leaves for India 66
Posted to Campbellpore 69

Staff-captain, Abbottabad 95
Posted to Rawalpindi 99
Leaves Royal Artillery 109
Joins Indian Army 110
Stationed at Ferozepore 110
Posted to Lahore 131
Posted to Rawalpindi (1931) 145
At Mil. Coll. of Science, Woolwich 161
Outbreak of World War II 166
Sails to Basra 170
Service in Iraq 172-183
Returns India, posted to Chaklala 183
Serves at HQ, 15th Indian Corps, Calcutta 184-8
Posted to Ranchi 188
Posted to Quetta 193
Resigns from Army, settles in S.A. 199
Secretary, 1820 Settlers Assn. 199
Hodgson, Mrs. Clarence 42, 44, 46-7, 57-8, 65-6, 68, 73, 75, 82, 90, 94, 96-7, 104, 111-113, 116-7, 119, 120, 126, 129, 130, 133, 142, 144, 157, 164, 166, 183, 190, 191, 194, 197-8
Hodgson, Mrs. Frederick (mother) 13, 14, 32-3, 44, 46-7, 128-9, 130
Hodgson Leslie 32, 157
Hodgson, Victor (twin) 8, 9, 32
Holdhurst forest 27
Hollywood (Ireland) 42
Hooghly river 185
Howrah 186
Huns (see Germans)
Hythe 161, 163

I
Imphal 186-7
India 10, 51, 55, 66, 68-9, 70-100, 102-128, 130-131, 133-5, 157-8, 160-1, 176, 178, 184-6, 190-1, 193-200